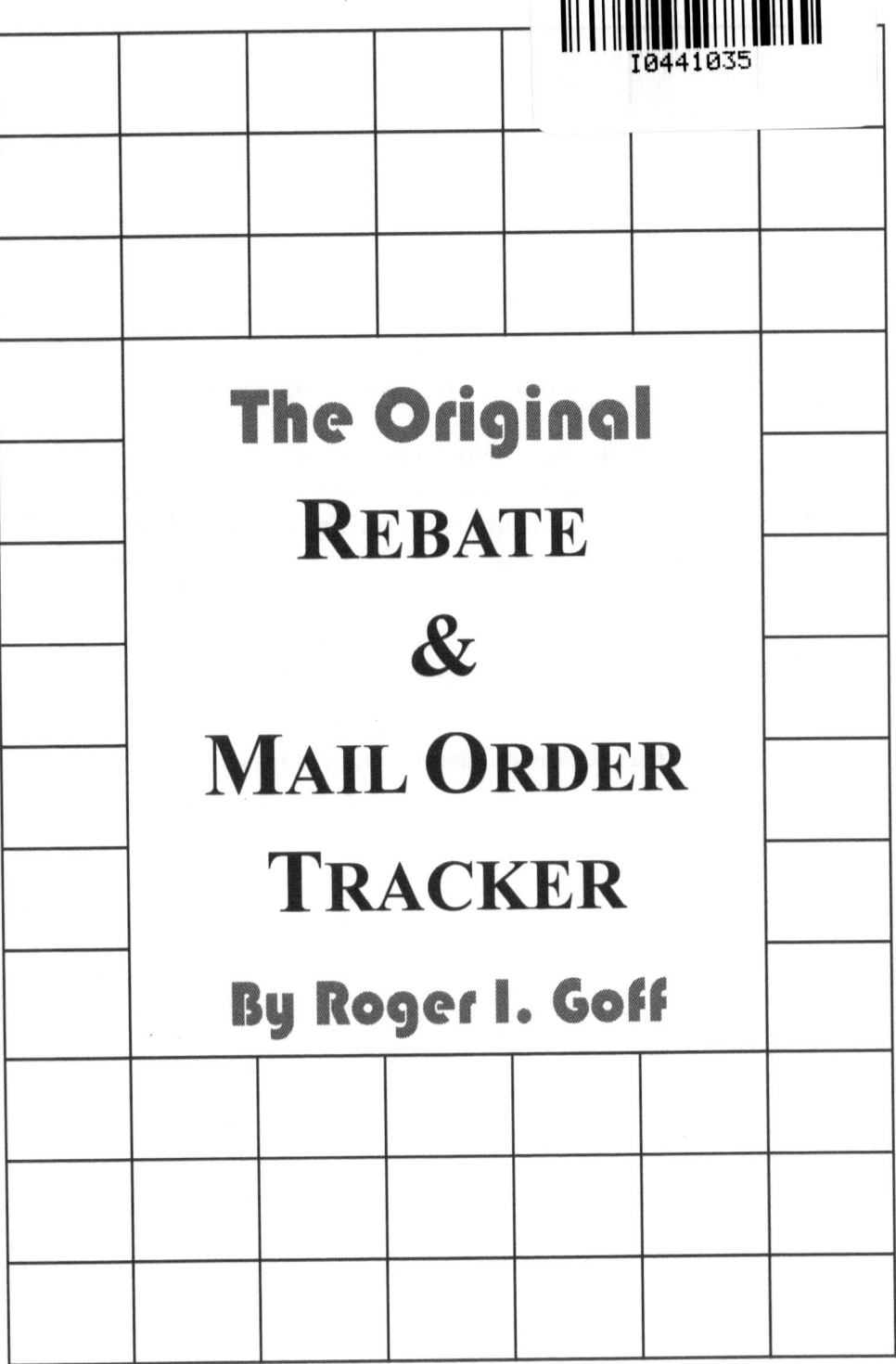

The Original
REBATE
&
MAIL ORDER
TRACKER

By Roger I. Goff

ISBN: 0-75964-016-5

This book is printed on acid free paper.

1stBooks – rev. 05/25/01

Contents

About the Book vii

From the Author ix

Chapter 1　The Three Dimensional Economic Estimates 1

Chapter 2　The Human Resource in a
　　　　　　Three-Dimensional Economic Space 14

Chapter 3　The Problems of Construction of the Economic Theory
　　　　　　of the Intellectual Sphere 20

Chapter 4　The Movement of Intellectual Values, Intellectual Services and
　　　　　　of the Aggregate Intellectual Product 27

Chapter 5　The Economic Estimations of the Services of the «Educational»,
　　　　　　«Enlightenment» and «Entertainment» Branches
　　　　　　Including A_{STP} 36

Chapter 6　The Economic Estimates, Criteria and Indicators
　　　　　　of the Movement of the Services of Education,
　　　　　　Enlightenment and Entertainment in Economic Space 46

Chapter 7　The Peculiarities of the Reproduction
　　　　　　of the Intellectual Sphere 61

Chapter 8　The Reproduction of the Entertainment Sphere 81

Chapter 9　The Proportions as a System of Economic Estimations
　　　　　　of Distribution 89

Chapter 10   The System of the Criteria of Intellectual Provision
(With Complex Numbers—Quaternions) 102

Chapter 11   The Economic Arithmetic's in Intellectual Sphere Taking
into Account of Services of the Three Branches of Power.......... 135

Part 2
The Intellectual Sphere of the USA

Chapter 1   The Economic Parameters of the Branches
of Intellectual Production Division I 177

Chapter 2   The Economic Parameters of the Branches
of Intellectual Production in the USA Divisions II & III 192

About the Author 225

The Liberty Index

Sergey Khrystenko

iUniverse, Inc.
New York Lincoln Shanghai

The Liberty Index

iUniverse books may be ordered through booksellers or by contacting:

iUniverse
2021 Pine Lake Road, Suite 100
Lincoln, NE 68512
www.iuniverse.com
1-800-Authors (1-800-288-4677)

ISBN: 978-0-595-43412-1 (pbk)
ISBN: 978-0-595-87736-2 (ebk)

Printed in the United States of America

THANK YOU FOR PURCHASING THE ORIGINAL REBATE AND MAIL ORDER TRACKER. YOUR PURCHASE WILL PAY FOR ITSELF MANY TIMES OVER. REMEMBER, REBATES AND MAIL ORDERS DO BECOME LOST IN TRANSIT. WHY DON'T YOU PROTECT YOURSELF BY RECORDING THEM IN "THE TRACKER."

TWO (2) SAMPLES HAVE BEEN PROVIDED TO DEMONSTRATE JUST HOW EASY IT IS TO USE "THE TRACKER." ONE IS FOR REBATES AND ONE IS FOR MAIL ORDERS.

QUICK TIPS:

FILL IN THE DATE PROMPTLY WHEN YOU RECEIVE YOUR REBATE/MAIL ORDER. MARK THE DATE IN RED. THIS MAKES IT EASIER TO CHECK ON IN THE FUTURE.

NOT EVERYONE SENDS IN THEIR REBATES IMMEDIATELY. IF YOU DELAY SENDING IT IN FOR MORE THAN ONE WEEK, A DATE SENT LINE IS PROVIDED FOR YOUR ACCURACY. THIS GIVES YOU A TRUER IDEA OF HOW LONG YOU HAVE WAITED.

SOMETIMES A TOLL-FREE NUMBER AND/OR AN INTERNET ADDRESS IS PROVIDED TO CHECK ON YOUR REBATE. THE MANUFACTURER MAY ALSO STATE A TIME FRAME ON HOW LONG IT WILL TAKE TO RECEIVE YOUR REBATE. THERE ARE LINES IN "THE TRACKER" FOR THIS INFORMATION.

THANK YOU,

ROGER I. GOFF

REBATE SAMPLE

Purchase Date: ___12/13/00___ Date Sent: ___12/25/00___

My Rebate/Mail Order was sent to:

Name ___Acme Media Plaza___

Address ___1234 North St.___

City ___Luckland___ State ___NY___

Zip Code ___12345-6789___

REBATE

I should be receiving $ ___45___ for buying:

___Magic 52 Speed CD Rom drive___

I received my rebate on: ___2/14/01___

Phone # to call after _____ weeks: _____

Or online at: _____

MAIL ORDER

My mail order purchase was for:

_____

The cost was $ _____ and the order was

received on _____

<hr>

MAIL ORDER SAMPLE

Purchase Date: ___10/24/00___ Date Sent _____

My Rebate/Mail Order was sent to:

Name ___Acme Book Market___

Address ___4321 South St.___

City ___Ladyluck___ State ___NY___

Zip Code ___43210___

REBATE

I should be receiving $ _____ for buying:

_____

I received my rebate on: _____

Phone # to call after _____ weeks: _____

Or online at: _____

MAIL ORDER

My mail order purchase was for:

___"White Socks Under My Bed"___

The cost was $ ___14.95___ and the order was

received on ___11/8/00___

1

Purchase Date: _____ Date Sent: _____
My Rebate/Mail Order was sent to:
Name _____
Address _____
City _____ State _____
Zip Code _____
REBATE
I should be receiving $_____ for buying:
_____
I received my rebate on: _____
Phone # to call after _____ weeks: _____
Or online at: _____
MAIL ORDER
My mail order purchase was for:
_____
The cost was $_____ and the order was
received on _____

■■■■■■■■■■■■■■■■■■■■■■■■■■■■■■■■■■■■

Purchase Date: _____ Date Sent _____
My Rebate/Mail Order was sent to:
Name _____
Address _____
City _____ State _____
Zip Code _____
REBATE
I should be receiving $_____ for buying:
_____
I received my rebate on: _____
Phone # to call after _____ weeks: _____
Or online at: _____
MAIL ORDER
My mail order purchase was for:
_____
The cost was $_____ and the order was
received on _____

Purchase Date: _____ Date Sent: _____
My Rebate/Mail Order was sent to:
Name _____
Address _____
City _____ State _____
                    Zip Code _____

REBATE
I should be receiving $_____ for buying:

_____
I received my rebate on: _____
Phone # to call after _____ weeks: _____
Or online at: _____
MAIL ORDER
My mail order purchase was for:

_____
The cost was $_____ and the order was
received on _____

■■■

Purchase Date: _____ Date Sent _____
My Rebate/Mail Order was sent to:
Name _____
Address _____
City _____ State _____
                    Zip Code _____

REBATE
I should be receiving $_____ for buying:

_____
I received my rebate on: _____
Phone # to call after _____ weeks: _____
Or online at: _____
MAIL ORDER
My mail order purchase was for:

_____
The cost was $_____ and the order was
received on _____

Purchase Date: _____ Date Sent: _____
My Rebate/Mail Order was sent to:
Name _____
Address _____
City _____ State _____
           Zip Code _____

REBATE
I should be receiving $_____ for buying:

_____
I received my rebate on: _____
 Phone # to call after _____ weeks: _____
Or online at: _____
MAIL ORDER
My mail order purchase was for:

The cost was $_____ and the order was
received on _____

■■■

Purchase Date: _____ Date Sent _____
My Rebate/Mail Order was sent to:
Name _____
Address _____
City _____ State _____
           Zip Code _____

REBATE
I should be receiving $_____ for buying:

_____
I received my rebate on: _____
 Phone # to call after _____ weeks: _____
Or online at: _____
MAIL ORDER
My mail order purchase was for:

The cost was $_____ and the order was
received on _____

4

Purchase Date: _____ Date Sent: _____
My Rebate/Mail Order was sent to:
Name _____
Address _____
City _____ State _____
                  Zip Code _____

REBATE
I should be receiving $ _____ for buying:
_____
I received my rebate on: _____
Phone # to call after _____ weeks: _____
Or online at: _____
MAIL ORDER
My mail order purchase was for:
_____
The cost was $ _____ and the order was
received on _____

▪▪

Purchase Date: _____ Date Sent _____
My Rebate/Mail Order was sent to:
Name _____
Address _____
City _____ State _____
                  Zip Code _____

REBATE
I should be receiving $ _____ for buying:
_____
I received my rebate on: _____
Phone # to call after _____ weeks: _____
Or online at: _____
MAIL ORDER
My mail order purchase was for:
_____
The cost was $ _____ and the order was
received on _____

Purchase Date: _____ Date Sent: _____

My Rebate/Mail Order was sent to:

Name _____

Address _____

City _____ State _____

Zip Code _____

REBATE

I should be receiving $_____ for buying:

_____

I received my rebate on: _____

Phone # to call after _____ weeks: _____

Or online at: _____

MAIL ORDER

My mail order purchase was for:

_____

The cost was $_____ and the order was

received on _____

■■■■■■■■■■■■■■■■■■■■■■■■■■■■■■■■■■■■

Purchase Date: _____ Date Sent _____

My Rebate/Mail Order was sent to:

Name _____

Address _____

City _____ State _____

Zip Code _____

REBATE

I should be receiving $_____ for buying:

_____

I received my rebate on: _____

Phone # to call after _____ weeks: _____

Or online at: _____

MAIL ORDER

My mail order purchase was for:

_____

The cost was $_____ and the order was

received on _____

Purchase Date: _____ Date Sent: _____
My Rebate/Mail Order was sent to:
Name _____
Address _____
City _____ State _____
                Zip Code _____

REBATE
I should be receiving $ _____ for buying:

_____
I received my rebate on: _____
Phone # to call after _____ weeks: _____
Or online at: _____
MAIL ORDER
My mail order purchase was for:

_____
The cost was $ _____ and the order was
received on _____

■■

Purchase Date: _____ Date Sent _____
My Rebate/Mail Order was sent to:
Name _____
Address _____
City _____ State _____
                Zip Code _____

REBATE
I should be receiving $ _____ for buying:

_____
I received my rebate on: _____
Phone # to call after _____ weeks: _____
Or online at: _____
MAIL ORDER
My mail order purchase was for:

_____
The cost was $ _____ and the order was
received on _____

Purchase Date: _____ Date Sent: _____

My Rebate/Mail Order was sent to:

Name _____

Address _____

City _____ State _____

Zip Code _____

REBATE

I should be receiving $_____ for buying:

_____

I received my rebate on: _____

Phone # to call after _____ weeks: _____

Or online at: _____

MAIL ORDER

My mail order purchase was for:

_____

The cost was $_____ and the order was

received on _____

■■

Purchase Date: _____ Date Sent _____

My Rebate/Mail Order was sent to:

Name _____

Address _____

City _____ State _____

Zip Code _____

REBATE

I should be receiving $_____ for buying:

_____

I received my rebate on: _____

Phone # to call after _____ weeks: _____

Or online at: _____

MAIL ORDER

My mail order purchase was for:

_____

The cost was $_____ and the order was

received on _____

Purchase Date: _____ Date Sent: _____
My Rebate/Mail Order was sent to:
Name _____
Address _____
City _____ State _____
Zip Code _____

REBATE
I should be receiving $_____ for buying:

_____
I received my rebate on: _____
Phone # to call after _____ weeks: _____
Or online at: _____
MAIL ORDER
My mail order purchase was for:

_____
The cost was $_____ and the order was
received on _____

■■■■■■■■■■■■■■■■■■■■■■■■■■■■■■■■■■■■■

Purchase Date: _____ Date Sent _____
My Rebate/Mail Order was sent to:
Name _____
Address _____
City _____ State _____
Zip Code _____

REBATE
I should be receiving $_____ for buying:

_____
I received my rebate on: _____
Phone # to call after _____ weeks: _____
Or online at: _____
MAIL ORDER
My mail order purchase was for:

_____
The cost was $_____ and the order was
received on _____

Purchase Date: _____ Date Sent: _____
My Rebate/Mail Order was sent to:
Name _____
Address _____
City _____ State _____
          Zip Code _____

REBATE

I should be receiving $ _____ for buying:

_____
I received my rebate on: _____
Phone # to call after _____ weeks: _____
Or online at: _____
MAIL ORDER
My mail order purchase was for:

_____
The cost was $ _____ and the order was
received on _____

▪▪

Purchase Date: _____ Date Sent _____
My Rebate/Mail Order was sent to:
Name _____
Address _____
City _____ State _____
          Zip Code _____

REBATE

I should be receiving $ _____ for buying:

_____
I received my rebate on: _____
Phone # to call after _____ weeks: _____
Or online at: _____
MAIL ORDER
My mail order purchase was for:

_____
The cost was $ _____ and the order was
received on _____

Purchase Date: _____ Date Sent: _____
My Rebate/Mail Order was sent to:
Name _____
Address _____
City _____ State _____
Zip Code _____

REBATE
I should be receiving $ _____ for buying:

_____
I received my rebate on: _____
Phone # to call after _____ weeks: _____
Or online at: _____
MAIL ORDER
My mail order purchase was for:

_____
The cost was $ _____ and the order was
received on _____

■■■■■■■■■■■■■■■■■■■■■■■■■■■■■■■■■■■■

Purchase Date: _____ Date Sent _____
My Rebate/Mail Order was sent to:
Name _____
Address _____
City _____ State _____
Zip Code _____

REBATE
I should be receiving $ _____ for buying:

_____
I received my rebate on: _____
Phone # to call after _____ weeks: _____
Or online at: _____
MAIL ORDER
My mail order purchase was for:

_____
The cost was $ _____ and the order was
received on _____

Purchase Date: _____ Date Sent: _____

My Rebate/Mail Order was sent to:

Name _____

Address _____

City _____ State _____

Zip Code _____

REBATE

I should be receiving $ _____ for buying:

_____

I received my rebate on: _____

Phone # to call after _____ weeks: _____

Or online at: _____

MAIL ORDER

My mail order purchase was for:

_____

The cost was $ _____ and the order was

received on _____

■■■

Purchase Date: _____ Date Sent _____

My Rebate/Mail Order was sent to:

Name _____

Address _____

City _____ State _____

Zip Code _____

REBATE

I should be receiving $ _____ for buying:

_____

I received my rebate on: _____

Phone # to call after _____ weeks: _____

Or online at: _____

MAIL ORDER

My mail order purchase was for:

_____

The cost was $ _____ and the order was

received on _____

Purchase Date: _____ Date Sent: _____
My Rebate/Mail Order was sent to:
Name _____
Address _____
City _____ State _____
Zip Code _____

REBATE
I should be receiving $_____ for buying:

_____
I received my rebate on: _____
Phone # to call after _____ weeks: _____
Or online at: _____
MAIL ORDER
My mail order purchase was for:

_____
The cost was $_____ and the order was
received on _____

█▪█▪█▪█▪█▪█▪█▪█▪█▪█▪█▪█▪█▪█▪█▪█▪█▪█▪█▪

Purchase Date: _____ Date Sent _____
My Rebate/Mail Order was sent to:
Name _____
Address _____
City _____ State _____
Zip Code _____

REBATE
I should be receiving $_____ for buying:

_____
I received my rebate on: _____
Phone # to call after _____ weeks: _____
Or online at: _____
MAIL ORDER
My mail order purchase was for:

_____
The cost was $_____ and the order was
received on _____

Purchase Date: _____ Date Sent: _____

My Rebate/Mail Order was sent to:

Name _____

Address _____

City _____ State _____

Zip Code _____

REBATE

I should be receiving $_____ for buying:

_____

I received my rebate on: _____

Phone # to call after _____ weeks: _____

Or online at: _____

MAIL ORDER

My mail order purchase was for:

_____

The cost was $_____ and the order was

received on _____

■□■□■□■□■□■□■□■□■□■□■□■□■□■□■□■□■□■□■□

Purchase Date: _____ Date Sent _____

My Rebate/Mail Order was sent to:

Name _____

Address _____

City _____ State _____

Zip Code _____

REBATE

I should be receiving $_____ for buying:

_____

I received my rebate on: _____

Phone # to call after _____ weeks: _____

Or online at: _____

MAIL ORDER

My mail order purchase was for:

_____

The cost was $_____ and the order was

received on _____

Purchase Date: _____ Date Sent: _____

My Rebate/Mail Order was sent to:

Name _____

Address _____

City _____ State _____

Zip Code _____

REBATE

I should be receiving $ _____ for buying:

_____

I received my rebate on: _____

Phone # to call after _____ weeks: _____

Or online at: _____

MAIL ORDER

My mail order purchase was for:

_____

The cost was $ _____ and the order was

received on _____

■■■■■■■■■■■■■■■■■■■■■■■■■■■■■■■■■■■■■■

Purchase Date: _____ Date Sent _____

My Rebate/Mail Order was sent to:

Name _____

Address _____

City _____ State _____

Zip Code _____

REBATE

I should be receiving $ _____ for buying:

_____

I received my rebate on: _____

Phone # to call after _____ weeks: _____

Or online at: _____

MAIL ORDER

My mail order purchase was for:

_____

The cost was $ _____ and the order was

received on _____

15

Purchase Date: _____ Date Sent: _____
My Rebate/Mail Order was sent to:
Name _____
Address _____
City _____ State _____
Zip Code _____

REBATE
I should be receiving $_____ for buying:

_____
I received my rebate on: _____
 Phone # to call after _____ weeks: _____
Or online at: _____
MAIL ORDER
My mail order purchase was for:

_____
The cost was $_____ and the order was
received on _____

■■■

Purchase Date: _____ Date Sent _____
My Rebate/Mail Order was sent to:
Name _____
Address _____
City _____ State _____
Zip Code _____

REBATE
I should be receiving $_____ for buying:

_____
I received my rebate on: _____
 Phone # to call after _____ weeks: _____
Or online at: _____
MAIL ORDER
My mail order purchase was for:

_____
The cost was $_____ and the order was
received on _____

Purchase Date: _____ Date Sent: _____
My Rebate/Mail Order was sent to:
Name _____
Address _____
City _____ State _____
Zip Code _____

REBATE
I should be receiving $_____ for buying:

_____
I received my rebate on: _____
Phone # to call after _____ weeks: _____
Or online at: _____
MAIL ORDER
My mail order purchase was for:

_____
The cost was $_____ and the order was
received on _____

■■■

Purchase Date: _____ Date Sent _____
My Rebate/Mail Order was sent to:
Name _____
Address _____
City _____ State _____
Zip Code _____

REBATE
I should be receiving $_____ for buying:

_____
I received my rebate on: _____
Phone # to call after _____ weeks: _____
Or online at: _____
MAIL ORDER
My mail order purchase was for:

_____
The cost was $_____ and the order was
received on _____

Purchase Date: _____ Date Sent: _____

My Rebate/Mail Order was sent to:

Name _____

Address _____

City _____ State _____

Zip Code _____

REBATE

I should be receiving $ _____ for buying:

_____

I received my rebate on: _____

Phone # to call after _____ weeks: _____

Or online at: _____

MAIL ORDER

My mail order purchase was for:

_____

The cost was $ _____ and the order was

received on _____

■:■■■■■■■■■■■■■■■■■■■■■■■■■■■■■■■■■■■■■■■

Purchase Date: _____ Date Sent _____

My Rebate/Mail Order was sent to:

Name _____

Address _____

City _____ State _____

Zip Code _____

REBATE

I should be receiving $ _____ for buying:

_____

I received my rebate on: _____

Phone # to call after _____ weeks: _____

Or online at: _____

MAIL ORDER

My mail order purchase was for:

_____

The cost was $ _____ and the order was

received on _____

Purchase Date: _____ Date Sent: _____
My Rebate/Mail Order was sent to:
Name _____
Address _____
City _____ State _____
                    Zip Code _____

REBATE
I should be receiving $_____ for buying:
_____
I received my rebate on: _____
Phone # to call after _____ weeks: _____
Or online at: _____
MAIL ORDER
My mail order purchase was for:
_____
The cost was $_____ and the order was
received on _____

▪▪▪▪▪▪▪▪▪▪▪▪▪▪▪▪▪▪▪▪▪▪▪▪▪▪▪▪▪▪▪▪▪▪▪▪▪

Purchase Date: _____ Date Sent _____
My Rebate/Mail Order was sent to:
Name _____
Address _____
City _____ State _____
                    Zip Code _____

REBATE
I should be receiving $_____ for buying:
_____
I received my rebate on: _____
Phone # to call after _____ weeks: _____
Or online at: _____
MAIL ORDER
My mail order purchase was for:
_____
The cost was $_____ and the order was
received on _____

Purchase Date: _____ Date Sent: _____

My Rebate/Mail Order was sent to:

Name _____

Address _____

City _____ State _____

Zip Code _____

REBATE

I should be receiving $_____ for buying:

_____

I received my rebate on: _____

 Phone # to call after _____ weeks: _____

Or online at: _____

MAIL ORDER

My mail order purchase was for:

_____

The cost was $_____ and the order was

received on _____

■■

Purchase Date: _____ Date Sent _____

My Rebate/Mail Order was sent to:

Name _____

Address _____

City _____ State _____

Zip Code _____

REBATE

I should be receiving $_____ for buying:

_____

I received my rebate on: _____

 Phone # to call after _____ weeks: _____

Or online at: _____

MAIL ORDER

My mail order purchase was for:

_____

The cost was $_____ and the order was

received on _____

Purchase Date: _____ Date Sent: _____

My Rebate/Mail Order was sent to:

Name _____

Address _____

City _____ State _____

Zip Code _____

REBATE

I should be receiving $ _____ for buying:

_____

I received my rebate on: _____

Phone # to call after _____ weeks: _____

Or online at: _____

MAIL ORDER

My mail order purchase was for:

_____

The cost was $ _____ and the order was

received on _____

▪▪▪▪▪▪▪▪▪▪▪▪▪▪▪▪▪▪▪▪▪▪▪▪▪▪▪▪▪▪▪▪▪▪▪▪▪▪▪

Purchase Date: _____ Date Sent _____

My Rebate/Mail Order was sent to:

Name _____

Address _____

City _____ State _____

Zip Code _____

REBATE

I should be receiving $ _____ for buying:

_____

I received my rebate on: _____

Phone # to call after _____ weeks: _____

Or online at: _____

MAIL ORDER

My mail order purchase was for:

_____

The cost was $ _____ and the order was

received on _____

Purchase Date: _____ Date Sent: _____

My Rebate/Mail Order was sent to:

Name _____

Address _____

City _____ State _____

Zip Code _____

REBATE

I should be receiving $ _____ for buying:

_____

I received my rebate on: _____

Phone # to call after _____ weeks: _____

Or online at: _____

MAIL ORDER

My mail order purchase was for:

_____

The cost was $ _____ and the order was

received on _____

■■■

Purchase Date: _____ Date Sent _____

My Rebate/Mail Order was sent to:

Name _____

Address _____

City _____ State _____

Zip Code _____

REBATE

I should be receiving $ _____ for buying:

_____

I received my rebate on: _____

Phone # to call after _____ weeks: _____

Or online at: _____

MAIL ORDER

My mail order purchase was for:

_____

The cost was $ _____ and the order was

received on _____

Purchase Date: _____ Date Sent: _____

My Rebate/Mail Order was sent to:

Name _____

Address _____

City _____ State _____

Zip Code _____

REBATE

I should be receiving $_____ for buying:

_____

I received my rebate on: _____

Phone # to call after _____ weeks: _____

Or online at: _____

MAIL ORDER

My mail order purchase was for:

_____

The cost was $_____ and the order was

received on _____

▪▪▪▪▪▪▪▪▪▪▪▪▪▪▪▪▪▪▪▪▪▪▪▪▪▪▪▪▪▪▪▪▪▪▪▪▪▪▪

Purchase Date: _____ Date Sent _____

My Rebate/Mail Order was sent to:

Name _____

Address _____

City _____ State _____

Zip Code _____

REBATE

I should be receiving $_____ for buying:

_____

I received my rebate on: _____

Phone # to call after _____ weeks: _____

Or online at: _____

MAIL ORDER

My mail order purchase was for:

_____

The cost was $_____ and the order was

received on _____

Purchase Date: _____ Date Sent: _____

My Rebate/Mail Order was sent to:

Name _____

Address _____

City _____ State _____

Zip Code _____

REBATE

I should be receiving $_____ for buying:

_____

I received my rebate on: _____

Phone # to call after _____ weeks: _____

Or online at: _____

MAIL ORDER

My mail order purchase was for:

_____

The cost was $_____ and the order was

received on _____

■■■■■■■■■■■■■■■■■■■■■■■■■■■■■■■■■■■■■■

Purchase Date: _____ Date Sent _____

My Rebate/Mail Order was sent to:

Name _____

Address _____

City _____ State _____

Zip Code _____

REBATE

I should be receiving $_____ for buying:

_____

I received my rebate on: _____

Phone # to call after _____ weeks: _____

Or online at: _____

MAIL ORDER

My mail order purchase was for:

_____

The cost was $_____ and the order was

received on _____

Purchase Date: _____ Date Sent: _____
My Rebate/Mail Order was sent to:
Name _____
Address _____
City _____ State _____
                Zip Code _____

REBATE
I should be receiving $_____ for buying:
_____
I received my rebate on: _____
Phone # to call after _____ weeks: _____
Or online at: _____
MAIL ORDER
My mail order purchase was for:
_____
The cost was $_____ and the order was
received on _____

■■■■■■■■■■■■■■■■■■■■■■■■■■■■■■■■■■■■■■

Purchase Date: _____ Date Sent _____
My Rebate/Mail Order was sent to:
Name _____
Address _____
City _____ State _____
                Zip Code _____

REBATE
I should be receiving $_____ for buying:
_____
I received my rebate on: _____
Phone # to call after _____ weeks: _____
Or online at: _____
MAIL ORDER
My mail order purchase was for:
_____
The cost was $_____ and the order was
received on _____

Purchase Date: _____ Date Sent: _____

My Rebate/Mail Order was sent to:

Name _____

Address _____

City _____ State _____

Zip Code _____

REBATE

I should be receiving $_____ for buying:

_____

I received my rebate on: _____

 Phone # to call after _____ weeks: _____

Or online at: _____

MAIL ORDER

My mail order purchase was for:

_____

The cost was $_____ and the order was

received on _____

▪▪▪

Purchase Date: _____ Date Sent _____

My Rebate/Mail Order was sent to:

Name _____

Address _____

City _____ State _____

Zip Code _____

REBATE

I should be receiving $_____ for buying:

_____

I received my rebate on: _____

 Phone # to call after _____ weeks: _____

Or online at: _____

MAIL ORDER

My mail order purchase was for:

_____

The cost was $_____ and the order was

received on _____

Purchase Date: _____ Date Sent: _____

My Rebate/Mail Order was sent to:

Name _____

Address _____

City _____ State _____

Zip Code _____

REBATE

I should be receiving $_____ for buying:

_____

I received my rebate on: _____

Phone # to call after _____ weeks: _____

Or online at: _____

MAIL ORDER

My mail order purchase was for:

_____

The cost was $_____ and the order was

received on _____

■■

Purchase Date: _____ Date Sent _____

My Rebate/Mail Order was sent to:

Name _____

Address _____

City _____ State _____

Zip Code _____

REBATE

I should be receiving $_____ for buying:

_____

I received my rebate on: _____

Phone # to call after _____ weeks: _____

Or online at: _____

MAIL ORDER

My mail order purchase was for:

_____

The cost was $_____ and the order was

received on _____

Purchase Date: _____ Date Sent: _____

My Rebate/Mail Order was sent to:

Name _____

Address _____

City _____ State _____

Zip Code _____

REBATE

I should be receiving $ _____ for buying:

_____

I received my rebate on: _____

Phone # to call after _____ weeks: _____

Or online at: _____

MAIL ORDER

My mail order purchase was for:

_____

The cost was $ _____ and the order was
received on _____

■■

Purchase Date: _____ Date Sent _____

My Rebate/Mail Order was sent to:

Name _____

Address _____

City _____ State _____

Zip Code _____

REBATE

I should be receiving $ _____ for buying:

_____

I received my rebate on: _____

Phone # to call after _____ weeks: _____

Or online at: _____

MAIL ORDER

My mail order purchase was for:

_____

The cost was $ _____ and the order was
received on _____

Purchase Date: _____ Date Sent: _____
My Rebate/Mail Order was sent to:
Name _____
Address _____
City _____ State _____
　　　　　　　Zip Code _____

REBATE
I should be receiving $_____ for buying:

_____
I received my rebate on: _____
Phone # to call after _____ weeks: _____
Or online at: _____
MAIL ORDER
My mail order purchase was for:

_____
The cost was $_____ and the order was
received on _____

Purchase Date: _____ Date Sent _____
My Rebate/Mail Order was sent to:
Name _____
Address _____
City _____ State _____
　　　　　　　Zip Code _____

REBATE
I should be receiving $_____ for buying:

_____
I received my rebate on: _____
Phone # to call after _____ weeks: _____
Or online at: _____
MAIL ORDER
My mail order purchase was for:

_____
The cost was $_____ and the order was
received on _____

Purchase Date: _____ Date Sent: _____
My Rebate/Mail Order was sent to:
Name _____
Address _____
City _____ State _____
                    Zip Code _____
REBATE
I should be receiving $_____ for buying:

_____
I received my rebate on: _____
 Phone # to call after _____ weeks: _____
Or online at: _____
MAIL ORDER
My mail order purchase was for:

_____
The cost was $_____ and the order was
received on _____

▪▪▪

Purchase Date: _____ Date Sent _____
My Rebate/Mail Order was sent to:
Name _____
Address _____
City _____ State _____
                    Zip Code _____
REBATE
I should be receiving $_____ for buying:

_____
I received my rebate on: _____
 Phone # to call after _____ weeks: _____
Or online at: _____
MAIL ORDER
My mail order purchase was for:

_____
The cost was $_____ and the order was
received on _____

Purchase Date: _____ Date Sent: _____
My Rebate/Mail Order was sent to:
Name _____
Address _____
City _____ State _____
                  Zip Code _____

REBATE
I should be receiving $_____ for buying:

_____
I received my rebate on: _____
Phone # to call after _____ weeks: _____
Or online at: _____
MAIL ORDER
My mail order purchase was for:

_____
The cost was $_____ and the order was
received on _____

■■■■■■■■■■■■■■■■■■■■■■■■■■■■■■■■■■■■■

Purchase Date: _____ Date Sent _____
My Rebate/Mail Order was sent to:
Name _____
Address _____
City _____ State _____
                  Zip Code _____

REBATE
I should be receiving $_____ for buying:

_____
I received my rebate on: _____
Phone # to call after _____ weeks: _____
Or online at: _____
MAIL ORDER
My mail order purchase was for:

_____
The cost was $_____ and the order was
received on _____

Purchase Date: _____ Date Sent: _____

My Rebate/Mail Order was sent to:

Name _____

Address _____

City _____ State _____

Zip Code _____

REBATE

I should be receiving $_____ for buying:

_____

I received my rebate on: _____

Phone # to call after _____ weeks: _____

Or online at: _____

MAIL ORDER

My mail order purchase was for:

_____

The cost was $_____ and the order was

received on _____

∎∎∎∎∎∎∎∎∎∎∎∎∎∎∎∎∎∎∎∎∎∎∎∎∎∎∎∎∎∎∎∎∎

Purchase Date: _____ Date Sent _____

My Rebate/Mail Order was sent to:

Name _____

Address _____

City _____ State _____

Zip Code _____

REBATE

I should be receiving $_____ for buying:

_____

I received my rebate on: _____

Phone # to call after _____ weeks: _____

Or online at: _____

MAIL ORDER

My mail order purchase was for:

_____

The cost was $_____ and the order was

received on _____

Purchase Date: _____ Date Sent: _____
My Rebate/Mail Order was sent to:
Name _____
Address _____
City _____ State _____
                Zip Code _____

REBATE
I should be receiving $_____ for buying:

_____
I received my rebate on: _____
Phone # to call after _____ weeks: _____
Or online at: _____
MAIL ORDER
My mail order purchase was for:

_____
The cost was $_____ and the order was
received on _____

▮▮▮▮▮▮▮▮▮▮▮▮▮▮▮▮▮▮▮▮▮▮▮▮▮▮▮▮▮▮▮▮

Purchase Date: _____ Date Sent _____
My Rebate/Mail Order was sent to:
Name _____
Address _____
City _____ State _____
                Zip Code _____

REBATE
I should be receiving $_____ for buying:

_____
I received my rebate on: _____
Phone # to call after _____ weeks: _____
Or online at: _____
MAIL ORDER
My mail order purchase was for:

_____
The cost was $_____ and the order was
received on _____

Purchase Date: _____ Date Sent: _____

My Rebate/Mail Order was sent to:

Name _____

Address _____

City _____ State _____

Zip Code _____

REBATE

I should be receiving $ _____ for buying:

_____

I received my rebate on: _____

Phone # to call after _____ weeks: _____

Or online at: _____

MAIL ORDER

My mail order purchase was for:

_____

The cost was $ _____ and the order was

received on _____

▪▪

Purchase Date: _____ Date Sent _____

My Rebate/Mail Order was sent to:

Name _____

Address _____

City _____ State _____

Zip Code _____

REBATE

I should be receiving $ _____ for buying:

_____

I received my rebate on: _____

Phone # to call after _____ weeks: _____

Or online at: _____

MAIL ORDER

My mail order purchase was for:

_____

The cost was $ _____ and the order was

received on _____

Purchase Date: _____ Date Sent: _____
My Rebate/Mail Order was sent to:
Name _____
Address _____
City _____ State _____
Zip Code _____

REBATE
I should be receiving $_____ for buying:

_____

I received my rebate on: _____
Phone # to call after _____ weeks: _____
Or online at: _____
MAIL ORDER
My mail order purchase was for:

_____

The cost was $_____ and the order was
received on _____

■■■

Purchase Date: _____ Date Sent _____
My Rebate/Mail Order was sent to:
Name _____
Address _____
City _____ State _____
Zip Code _____

REBATE
I should be receiving $_____ for buying:

_____

I received my rebate on: _____
Phone # to call after _____ weeks: _____
Or online at: _____
MAIL ORDER
My mail order purchase was for:

_____

The cost was $_____ and the order was
received on _____

Purchase Date: _____ Date Sent: _____
My Rebate/Mail Order was sent to:
Name _____
Address _____
City _____ State _____
Zip Code _____
REBATE
I should be receiving $ _____ for buying:

_____
I received my rebate on: _____
Phone # to call after _____ weeks: _____
Or online at: _____
MAIL ORDER
My mail order purchase was for:

_____
The cost was $ _____ and the order was
received on _____

▪▪▪▪▪▪▪▪▪▪▪▪▪▪▪▪▪▪▪▪▪▪▪▪▪▪▪▪▪▪▪▪▪▪▪▪▪▪

Purchase Date: _____ Date Sent _____
My Rebate/Mail Order was sent to:
Name _____
Address _____
City _____ State _____
Zip Code _____
REBATE
I should be receiving $ _____ for buying:

_____
I received my rebate on: _____
Phone # to call after _____ weeks: _____
Or online at: _____
MAIL ORDER
My mail order purchase was for:

_____
The cost was $ _____ and the order was
received on _____

Purchase Date: _____ Date Sent: _____
My Rebate/Mail Order was sent to:
Name _____
Address _____
City _____ State _____
Zip Code _____

REBATE
I should be receiving $_____ for buying:
_____
I received my rebate on: _____
Phone # to call after _____ weeks: _____
Or online at: _____
MAIL ORDER
My mail order purchase was for:
_____
The cost was $_____ and the order was
received on _____

■■

Purchase Date: _____ Date Sent _____
My Rebate/Mail Order was sent to:
Name _____
Address _____
City _____ State _____
Zip Code _____

REBATE
I should be receiving $_____ for buying:
_____
I received my rebate on: _____
Phone # to call after _____ weeks: _____
Or online at: _____
MAIL ORDER
My mail order purchase was for:
_____
The cost was $_____ and the order was
received on _____

Purchase Date: _____ Date Sent: _____
My Rebate/Mail Order was sent to:
Name _____
Address _____
City _____ State _____
Zip Code _____

REBATE
I should be receiving $_____ for buying:

_____
I received my rebate on: _____
Phone # to call after _____ weeks: _____
Or online at: _____
MAIL ORDER
My mail order purchase was for:

_____
The cost was $_____ and the order was
received on _____

██

Purchase Date: _____ Date Sent _____
My Rebate/Mail Order was sent to:
Name _____
Address _____
City _____ State _____
Zip Code _____

REBATE
I should be receiving $_____ for buying:

_____
I received my rebate on: _____
Phone # to call after _____ weeks: _____
Or online at: _____
MAIL ORDER
My mail order purchase was for:

_____
The cost was $_____ and the order was
received on _____

Purchase Date: _____ Date Sent: _____

My Rebate/Mail Order was sent to:

Name _____

Address _____

City _____ State _____

Zip Code _____

REBATE

I should be receiving $_____ for buying:

_____

I received my rebate on: _____

Phone # to call after _____ weeks: _____

Or online at: _____

MAIL ORDER

My mail order purchase was for:

_____

The cost was $_____ and the order was

received on _____

▪▪▪▪▪▪▪▪▪▪▪▪▪▪▪▪▪▪▪▪▪▪▪▪▪▪▪▪▪▪▪▪▪▪▪▪▪

Purchase Date: _____ Date Sent _____

My Rebate/Mail Order was sent to:

Name _____

Address _____

City _____ State _____

Zip Code _____

REBATE

I should be receiving $_____ for buying:

_____

I received my rebate on: _____

Phone # to call after _____ weeks: _____

Or online at: _____

MAIL ORDER

My mail order purchase was for:

_____

The cost was $_____ and the order was

received on _____

Purchase Date: _____ Date Sent: _____
My Rebate/Mail Order was sent to:
Name _____
Address _____
City _____ State _____
                    Zip Code _____
REBATE
I should be receiving $ _____ for buying:

_____
I received my rebate on: _____
 Phone # to call after _____ weeks: _____
Or online at: _____
MAIL ORDER
My mail order purchase was for:

_____
The cost was $ _____ and the order was
received on   _____

■■■

Purchase Date: _____ Date Sent _____
My Rebate/Mail Order was sent to:
Name _____
Address _____
City _____ State _____
                    Zip Code _____
REBATE
I should be receiving $ _____ for buying:

_____
I received my rebate on: _____
 Phone # to call after _____ weeks: _____
Or online at: _____
MAIL ORDER
My mail order purchase was for:

_____
The cost was $ _____ and the order was
received on   _____

Purchase Date: _____ Date Sent: _____
My Rebate/Mail Order was sent to:
Name _____
Address _____
City _____ State _____
Zip Code _____

REBATE
I should be receiving $_____ for buying:
_____
I received my rebate on: _____
Phone # to call after _____ weeks: _____
Or online at: _____
MAIL ORDER
My mail order purchase was for:
_____
The cost was $_____ and the order was
received on _____

Purchase Date: _____ Date Sent _____
My Rebate/Mail Order was sent to:
Name _____
Address _____
City _____ State _____
Zip Code _____

REBATE
I should be receiving $_____ for buying:
_____
I received my rebate on: _____
Phone # to call after _____ weeks: _____
Or online at: _____
MAIL ORDER
My mail order purchase was for:
_____
The cost was $_____ and the order was
received on _____

Purchase Date: _____ Date Sent: _____
My Rebate/Mail Order was sent to:
Name _____
Address _____
City _____ State _____
Zip Code _____

REBATE
I should be receiving $_____ for buying:

_____
I received my rebate on: _____
Phone # to call after _____ weeks: _____
Or online at: _____
MAIL ORDER
My mail order purchase was for:

_____
The cost was $_____ and the order was
received on _____

■■■■■■■■■■■■■■■■■■■■■■■■■■■■■■■■■■■■

Purchase Date: _____ Date Sent _____
My Rebate/Mail Order was sent to:
Name _____
Address _____
City _____ State _____
Zip Code _____

REBATE
I should be receiving $_____ for buying:

_____
I received my rebate on: _____
Phone # to call after _____ weeks: _____
Or online at: _____
MAIL ORDER
My mail order purchase was for:

_____
The cost was $_____ and the order was
received on _____

Purchase Date: _____ Date Sent: _____
My Rebate/Mail Order was sent to:
Name _____
Address _____
City _____ State _____
              Zip Code _____

REBATE
I should be receiving $_____ for buying:

_____
I received my rebate on: _____
Phone # to call after _____ weeks: _____
Or online at: _____
MAIL ORDER
My mail order purchase was for:

_____
The cost was $_____ and the order was
received on _____

█▪

Purchase Date: _____ Date Sent _____
My Rebate/Mail Order was sent to:
Name _____
Address _____
City _____ State _____
              Zip Code _____

REBATE
I should be receiving $_____ for buying:

_____
I received my rebate on: _____
Phone # to call after _____ weeks: _____
Or online at: _____
MAIL ORDER
My mail order purchase was for:

_____
The cost was $_____ and the order was
received on _____

Purchase Date: _____ Date Sent: _____

My Rebate/Mail Order was sent to:

Name _____

Address _____

City _____ State _____

Zip Code _____

REBATE

I should be receiving $_____ for buying:

_____

I received my rebate on: _____

 Phone # to call after _____ weeks: _____

Or online at: _____

MAIL ORDER

My mail order purchase was for:

_____

The cost was $_____ and the order was

received on _____

■■■■■■■■■■■■■■■■■■■■■■■■■■■■■■■■■■■

Purchase Date: _____ Date Sent _____

My Rebate/Mail Order was sent to:

Name _____

Address _____

City _____ State _____

Zip Code _____

REBATE

I should be receiving $_____ for buying:

_____

I received my rebate on: _____

 Phone # to call after _____ weeks: _____

Or online at: _____

MAIL ORDER

My mail order purchase was for:

_____

The cost was $_____ and the order was

received on _____

Purchase Date: _____ Date Sent: _____

My Rebate/Mail Order was sent to:

Name _____

Address _____

City _____ State _____

Zip Code _____

REBATE

I should be receiving $_____ for buying:

_____

I received my rebate on: _____

Phone # to call after _____ weeks: _____

Or online at: _____

MAIL ORDER

My mail order purchase was for:

_____

The cost was $_____ and the order was

received on _____

Purchase Date: _____ Date Sent _____

My Rebate/Mail Order was sent to:

Name _____

Address _____

City _____ State _____

Zip Code _____

REBATE

I should be receiving $_____ for buying:

_____

I received my rebate on: _____

Phone # to call after _____ weeks: _____

Or online at: _____

MAIL ORDER

My mail order purchase was for:

_____

The cost was $_____ and the order was

received on _____

Purchase Date: _____ Date Sent: _____
My Rebate/Mail Order was sent to:
Name _____
Address _____
City _____ State _____
Zip Code _____

REBATE
I should be receiving $ _____ for buying:

_____
I received my rebate on: _____
Phone # to call after _____ weeks: _____
Or online at: _____
MAIL ORDER
My mail order purchase was for:

_____
The cost was $ _____ and the order was
received on _____

∎∎∎∎∎∎∎∎∎∎∎∎∎∎∎∎∎∎∎∎∎∎∎∎∎∎∎∎∎∎∎∎∎∎∎∎∎∎

Purchase Date: _____ Date Sent _____
My Rebate/Mail Order was sent to:
Name _____
Address _____
City _____ State _____
Zip Code _____

REBATE
I should be receiving $ _____ for buying:

_____
I received my rebate on: _____
Phone # to call after _____ weeks: _____
Or online at: _____
MAIL ORDER
My mail order purchase was for:

_____
The cost was $ _____ and the order was
received on _____

Purchase Date: _____ Date Sent: _____
My Rebate/Mail Order was sent to:
Name _____
Address _____
City _____ State _____
Zip Code _____

REBATE
I should be receiving $_____ for buying:

_____
I received my rebate on: _____
Phone # to call after _____ weeks: _____
Or online at: _____
MAIL ORDER
My mail order purchase was for:

_____
The cost was $_____ and the order was
received on _____

■■■■■■■■■■■■■■■■■■■■■■■■■■■■■■■■■■■■■■

Purchase Date: _____ Date Sent _____
My Rebate/Mail Order was sent to:
Name _____
Address _____
City _____ State _____
Zip Code _____

REBATE
I should be receiving $_____ for buying:

_____
I received my rebate on: _____
Phone # to call after _____ weeks: _____
Or online at: _____
MAIL ORDER
My mail order purchase was for:

_____
The cost was $_____ and the order was
received on _____

Purchase Date: _____ Date Sent: _____
My Rebate/Mail Order was sent to:
Name _____
Address _____
City _____ State _____
Zip Code _____

REBATE
I should be receiving $_____ for buying:
_____
I received my rebate on: _____
Phone # to call after _____ weeks: _____
Or online at: _____
MAIL ORDER
My mail order purchase was for:
_____
The cost was $_____ and the order was
received on _____

■■■■■■■■■■■■■■■■■■■■■■■■■■■■■■■■■■■■■

Purchase Date: _____ Date Sent _____
My Rebate/Mail Order was sent to:
Name _____
Address _____
City _____ State _____
Zip Code _____

REBATE
I should be receiving $_____ for buying:
_____
I received my rebate on: _____
Phone # to call after _____ weeks: _____
Or online at: _____
MAIL ORDER
My mail order purchase was for:
_____
The cost was $_____ and the order was
received on _____

Purchase Date: _____ Date Sent: _____
My Rebate/Mail Order was sent to:
Name _____
Address _____
City _____ State _____
Zip Code _____
REBATE
I should be receiving $_____ for buying:

_____
I received my rebate on: _____
Phone # to call after _____ weeks: _____
Or online at: _____
MAIL ORDER
My mail order purchase was for:

_____
The cost was $_____ and the order was
received on _____

■■■

Purchase Date: _____ Date Sent _____
My Rebate/Mail Order was sent to:
Name _____
Address _____
City _____ State _____
Zip Code _____
REBATE
I should be receiving $_____ for buying:

_____
I received my rebate on: _____
Phone # to call after _____ weeks: _____
Or online at: _____
MAIL ORDER
My mail order purchase was for:

_____
The cost was $_____ and the order was
received on _____

Purchase Date: _____ Date Sent: _____
My Rebate/Mail Order was sent to:
Name _____
Address _____
City _____ State _____
          Zip Code _____
REBATE
I should be receiving $_____ for buying:

_____
I received my rebate on: _____
 Phone # to call after _____ weeks: _____
Or online at: _____
MAIL ORDER
My mail order purchase was for:

_____
The cost was $_____ and the order was
received on   _____

■■■■■■■■■■■■■■■■■■■■■■■■■■■■■■■■■■■■

Purchase Date: _____ Date Sent _____
My Rebate/Mail Order was sent to:
Name _____
Address _____
City _____ State _____
          Zip Code _____
REBATE
I should be receiving $_____ for buying:

_____
I received my rebate on: _____
 Phone # to call after _____ weeks: _____
Or online at: _____
MAIL ORDER
My mail order purchase was for:

_____
The cost was $_____ and the order was
received on   _____

Purchase Date: _____ Date Sent: _____

My Rebate/Mail Order was sent to:

Name _____

Address _____

City _____ State _____

Zip Code _____

REBATE

I should be receiving $_____ for buying:

_____

I received my rebate on: _____

Phone # to call after _____ weeks: _____

Or online at: _____

MAIL ORDER

My mail order purchase was for:

_____

The cost was $_____ and the order was

received on _____

▮▮▮▮▮▮▮▮▮▮▮▮▮▮▮▮▮▮▮▮▮▮▮▮▮▮▮▮▮▮▮▮

Purchase Date: _____ Date Sent _____

My Rebate/Mail Order was sent to:

Name _____

Address _____

City _____ State _____

Zip Code _____

REBATE

I should be receiving $_____ for buying:

_____

I received my rebate on: _____

Phone # to call after _____ weeks: _____

Or online at: _____

MAIL ORDER

My mail order purchase was for:

_____

The cost was $_____ and the order was

received on _____

Purchase Date: _____ Date Sent: _____

My Rebate/Mail Order was sent to:

Name _____

Address _____

City _____ State _____

Zip Code _____

REBATE

I should be receiving $ _____ for buying:

_____

I received my rebate on: _____

Phone # to call after _____ weeks: _____

Or online at: _____

MAIL ORDER

My mail order purchase was for:

_____

The cost was $ _____ and the order was

received on _____

■■■■■■■■■■■■■■■■■■■■■■■■■■■■■■■■■■

Purchase Date: _____ Date Sent _____

My Rebate/Mail Order was sent to:

Name _____

Address _____

City _____ State _____

Zip Code _____

REBATE

I should be receiving $ _____ for buying:

_____

I received my rebate on: _____

Phone # to call after _____ weeks: _____

Or online at: _____

MAIL ORDER

My mail order purchase was for:

_____

The cost was $ _____ and the order was

received on _____

Purchase Date: _____ Date Sent: _____

My Rebate/Mail Order was sent to:

Name _____

Address _____

City _____ State _____

Zip Code _____

REBATE

I should be receiving $_____ for buying:

_____

I received my rebate on: _____

Phone # to call after _____ weeks: _____

Or online at: _____

MAIL ORDER

My mail order purchase was for:

_____

The cost was $_____ and the order was

received on _____

▪▪▪▪▪▪▪▪▪▪▪▪▪▪▪▪▪▪▪▪▪▪▪▪▪▪▪▪▪▪▪▪▪▪▪▪▪▪

Purchase Date: _____ Date Sent _____

My Rebate/Mail Order was sent to:

Name _____

Address _____

City _____ State _____

Zip Code _____

REBATE

I should be receiving $_____ for buying:

_____

I received my rebate on: _____

Phone # to call after _____ weeks: _____

Or online at: _____

MAIL ORDER

My mail order purchase was for:

_____

The cost was $_____ and the order was

received on _____

Purchase Date: _____ Date Sent: _____
My Rebate/Mail Order was sent to:
Name _____
Address _____
City _____ State _____
               Zip Code _____
REBATE
I should be receiving $_____ for buying:

_____
I received my rebate on: _____
Phone # to call after _____ weeks: _____
Or online at: _____
MAIL ORDER
My mail order purchase was for:

_____
The cost was $_____ and the order was
received on _____

▮▮▮▮▮▮▮▮▮▮▮▮▮▮▮▮▮▮▮▮▮▮▮▮▮▮▮▮▮▮▮▮▮

Purchase Date: _____ Date Sent _____
My Rebate/Mail Order was sent to:
Name _____
Address _____
City _____ State _____
               Zip Code _____
REBATE
I should be receiving $_____ for buying:

_____
I received my rebate on: _____
Phone # to call after _____ weeks: _____
Or online at: _____
MAIL ORDER
My mail order purchase was for:

_____
The cost was $_____ and the order was
received on _____

Purchase Date: _____ Date Sent: _____
My Rebate/Mail Order was sent to:
Name _____
Address _____
City _____ State _____
                    Zip Code _____

REBATE
I should be receiving $_____ for buying:

_____
I received my rebate on: _____
Phone # to call after _____ weeks: _____
Or online at: _____
MAIL ORDER
My mail order purchase was for:

_____
The cost was $_____ and the order was
received on   _____

■■

Purchase Date: _____ Date Sent _____
My Rebate/Mail Order was sent to:
Name _____
Address _____
City _____ State _____
                    Zip Code _____

REBATE
I should be receiving $_____ for buying:

_____
I received my rebate on: _____
Phone # to call after _____ weeks: _____
Or online at: _____
MAIL ORDER
My mail order purchase was for:

_____
The cost was $_____ and the order was
received on   _____

Purchase Date: _____ Date Sent: _____
My Rebate/Mail Order was sent to:
Name _____
Address _____
City _____ State _____
Zip Code _____

REBATE
I should be receiving $ _____ for buying:

_____
I received my rebate on: _____
Phone # to call after _____ weeks: _____
Or online at: _____
MAIL ORDER
My mail order purchase was for:

_____
The cost was $ _____ and the order was
received on _____

▪▪▪▪▪▪▪▪▪▪▪▪▪▪▪▪▪▪▪▪▪▪▪▪▪▪▪▪▪▪▪▪▪▪▪▪

Purchase Date: _____ Date Sent _____
My Rebate/Mail Order was sent to:
Name _____
Address _____
City _____ State _____
Zip Code _____

REBATE
I should be receiving $ _____ for buying:

_____
I received my rebate on: _____
Phone # to call after _____ weeks: _____
Or online at: _____
MAIL ORDER
My mail order purchase was for:

_____
The cost was $ _____ and the order was
received on _____

Purchase Date: _____ Date Sent: _____

My Rebate/Mail Order was sent to:

Name _____

Address _____

City _____ State _____

Zip Code _____

REBATE

I should be receiving $_____ for buying:

_____

I received my rebate on: _____

Phone # to call after _____ weeks: _____

Or online at: _____

MAIL ORDER

My mail order purchase was for:

_____

The cost was $_____ and the order was

received on _____

━━━━━━━━━━━━━━━━━━━━━━━━━━━━━━━━━━━━━━━

Purchase Date: _____ Date Sent _____

My Rebate/Mail Order was sent to:

Name _____

Address _____

City _____ State _____

Zip Code _____

REBATE

I should be receiving $_____ for buying:

_____

I received my rebate on: _____

Phone # to call after _____ weeks: _____

Or online at: _____

MAIL ORDER

My mail order purchase was for:

_____

The cost was $_____ and the order was

received on _____

Purchase Date: _____ Date Sent: _____

My Rebate/Mail Order was sent to:

Name _____

Address _____

City _____ State _____

Zip Code _____

REBATE

I should be receiving $ _____ for buying:

_____

I received my rebate on: _____

Phone # to call after _____ weeks: _____

Or online at: _____

MAIL ORDER

My mail order purchase was for:

_____

The cost was $ _____ and the order was
received on _____

▪▪▪▪▪▪▪▪▪▪▪▪▪▪▪▪▪▪▪▪▪▪▪▪▪▪▪▪▪▪▪▪▪▪

Purchase Date: _____ Date Sent _____

My Rebate/Mail Order was sent to:

Name _____

Address _____

City _____ State _____

Zip Code _____

REBATE

I should be receiving $ _____ for buying:

_____

I received my rebate on: _____

Phone # to call after _____ weeks: _____

Or online at: _____

MAIL ORDER

My mail order purchase was for:

_____

The cost was $ _____ and the order was
received on _____

Purchase Date: _____ Date Sent: _____
My Rebate/Mail Order was sent to:
Name _____
Address _____
City _____ State _____
Zip Code _____

REBATE
I should be receiving $_____ for buying:

_____
I received my rebate on: _____
Phone # to call after _____ weeks: _____
Or online at: _____
MAIL ORDER
My mail order purchase was for:

_____
The cost was $_____ and the order was
received on _____

▪▪▪▪▪▪▪▪▪▪▪▪▪▪▪▪▪▪▪▪▪▪▪▪▪▪▪▪▪▪▪▪▪▪▪▪▪

Purchase Date: _____ Date Sent _____
My Rebate/Mail Order was sent to:
Name _____
Address _____
City _____ State _____
Zip Code _____

REBATE
I should be receiving $_____ for buying:

_____
I received my rebate on: _____
Phone # to call after _____ weeks: _____
Or online at: _____
MAIL ORDER
My mail order purchase was for:

_____
The cost was $_____ and the order was
received on _____

Purchase Date: _____ Date Sent: _____
My Rebate/Mail Order was sent to:
Name _____
Address _____
City _____ State _____
                    Zip Code _____
REBATE
I should be receiving $_____ for buying:
_____
I received my rebate on: _____
 Phone # to call after _____ weeks: _____
Or online at: _____
MAIL ORDER
My mail order purchase was for:
_____
The cost was $_____ and the order was
received on _____

■■■■■■■■■■■■■■■■■■■■■■■■■■■■■■■■■■■

Purchase Date: _____ Date Sent _____
My Rebate/Mail Order was sent to:
Name _____
Address _____
City _____ State _____
                    Zip Code _____
REBATE
I should be receiving $_____ for buying:
_____
I received my rebate on: _____
Phone # to call after _____ weeks: _____
Or online at: _____
MAIL ORDER
My mail order purchase was for:
_____
The cost was $_____ and the order was
received on _____

Purchase Date: _____ Date Sent: _____

My Rebate/Mail Order was sent to:

Name _____

Address _____

City _____ State _____

Zip Code _____

REBATE

I should be receiving $ _____ for buying:

_____

I received my rebate on: _____

Phone # to call after _____ weeks: _____

Or online at: _____

MAIL ORDER

My mail order purchase was for:

_____

The cost was $ _____ and the order was

received on _____

▪▪▪▪▪▪▪▪▪▪▪▪▪▪▪▪▪▪▪▪▪▪▪▪▪▪▪▪▪▪▪▪▪▪▪▪

Purchase Date: _____ Date Sent _____

My Rebate/Mail Order was sent to:

Name _____

Address _____

City _____ State _____

Zip Code _____

REBATE

I should be receiving $ _____ for buying:

_____

I received my rebate on: _____

Phone # to call after _____ weeks: _____

Or online at: _____

MAIL ORDER

My mail order purchase was for:

_____

The cost was $ _____ and the order was

received on _____

Purchase Date: _____ Date Sent: _____

My Rebate/Mail Order was sent to:

Name _____

Address _____

City _____ State _____

Zip Code _____

REBATE

I should be receiving $_____ for buying:

_____

I received my rebate on: _____

Phone # to call after _____ weeks: _____

Or online at: _____

MAIL ORDER

My mail order purchase was for:

_____

The cost was $_____ and the order was

received on _____

■■■■■■■■■■■■■■■■■■■■■■■■■■■■■■■■■■■■■■■

Purchase Date: _____ Date Sent _____

My Rebate/Mail Order was sent to:

Name _____

Address _____

City _____ State _____

Zip Code _____

REBATE

I should be receiving $_____ for buying:

_____

I received my rebate on: _____

Phone # to call after _____ weeks: _____

Or online at: _____

MAIL ORDER

My mail order purchase was for:

_____

The cost was $_____ and the order was

received on _____

Purchase Date: _____ Date Sent: _____

My Rebate/Mail Order was sent to:

Name _____

Address _____

City _____ State _____

Zip Code _____

REBATE

I should be receiving $_____ for buying:

_____

I received my rebate on: _____

Phone # to call after _____ weeks: _____

Or online at: _____

MAIL ORDER

My mail order purchase was for:

_____

The cost was $_____ and the order was

received on _____

■■

Purchase Date: _____ Date Sent _____

My Rebate/Mail Order was sent to:

Name _____

Address _____

City _____ State _____

Zip Code _____

REBATE

I should be receiving $_____ for buying:

_____

I received my rebate on: _____

Phone # to call after _____ weeks: _____

Or online at: _____

MAIL ORDER

My mail order purchase was for:

_____

The cost was $_____ and the order was

received on _____

Purchase Date: _____ Date Sent: _____
My Rebate/Mail Order was sent to:
Name _____
Address _____
City _____ State _____
Zip Code _____

REBATE
I should be receiving $_____ for buying:

_____
I received my rebate on: _____
Phone # to call after _____ weeks: _____
Or online at: _____
MAIL ORDER
My mail order purchase was for:

_____
The cost was $_____ and the order was
received on _____

■■■■■■■■■■■■■■■■■■■■■■■■■■■■■■■■■■■

Purchase Date: _____ Date Sent _____
My Rebate/Mail Order was sent to:
Name _____
Address _____
City _____ State _____
Zip Code _____

REBATE
I should be receiving $_____ for buying:

_____
I received my rebate on: _____
Phone # to call after _____ weeks: _____
Or online at: _____
MAIL ORDER
My mail order purchase was for:

_____
The cost was $_____ and the order was
received on

Purchase Date: _____ Date Sent: _____

My Rebate/Mail Order was sent to:

Name _____

Address _____

City _____ State _____

Zip Code _____

REBATE

I should be receiving $_____ for buying:

_____

I received my rebate on: _____

Phone # to call after _____ weeks: _____

Or online at: _____

MAIL ORDER

My mail order purchase was for:

_____

The cost was $_____ and the order was

received on _____

Purchase Date: _____ Date Sent _____

My Rebate/Mail Order was sent to:

Name _____

Address _____

City _____ State _____

Zip Code _____

REBATE

I should be receiving $_____ for buying:

_____

I received my rebate on: _____

Phone # to call after _____ weeks: _____

Or online at: _____

MAIL ORDER

My mail order purchase was for:

_____

The cost was $_____ and the order was

received on _____

Purchase Date: _____ Date Sent: _____

My Rebate/Mail Order was sent to:

Name _____

Address _____

City _____ State _____

Zip Code _____

REBATE

I should be receiving $_____ for buying:

_____

I received my rebate on: _____

Phone # to call after _____ weeks: _____

Or online at: _____

MAIL ORDER

My mail order purchase was for:

_____

The cost was $_____ and the order was

received on _____

▪▪▪▪▪▪▪▪▪▪▪▪▪▪▪▪▪▪▪▪▪▪▪▪▪▪▪▪▪▪▪▪▪▪

Purchase Date: _____ Date Sent _____

My Rebate/Mail Order was sent to:

Name _____

Address _____

City _____ State _____

Zip Code _____

REBATE

I should be receiving $_____ for buying:

_____

I received my rebate on: _____

Phone # to call after _____ weeks: _____

Or online at: _____

MAIL ORDER

My mail order purchase was for:

_____

The cost was $_____ and the order was

received on _____

Purchase Date: _____ Date Sent: _____
My Rebate/Mail Order was sent to:
Name _____
Address _____
City _____ State _____
                    Zip Code _____
REBATE
I should be receiving $ _____ for buying:

_____
I received my rebate on: _____
Phone # to call after _____ weeks: _____
Or online at: _____
MAIL ORDER
My mail order purchase was for:

_____
The cost was $ _____ and the order was
received on _____

■■

Purchase Date: _____ Date Sent _____
My Rebate/Mail Order was sent to:
Name _____
Address _____
City _____ State _____
                    Zip Code _____
REBATE
I should be receiving $ _____ for buying:

_____
I received my rebate on: _____
Phone # to call after _____ weeks: _____
Or online at: _____
MAIL ORDER
My mail order purchase was for:

_____
The cost was $ _____ and the order was
received on _____

Purchase Date: _____ Date Sent: _____

My Rebate/Mail Order was sent to:

Name _____

Address _____

City _____ State _____

Zip Code _____

REBATE

I should be receiving $_____ for buying:

_____

I received my rebate on: _____

Phone # to call after _____ weeks: _____

Or online at: _____

MAIL ORDER

My mail order purchase was for:

_____

The cost was $_____ and the order was

received on _____

■■

Purchase Date: _____ Date Sent _____

My Rebate/Mail Order was sent to:

Name _____

Address _____

City _____ State _____

Zip Code _____

REBATE

I should be receiving $_____ for buying:

_____

I received my rebate on: _____

Phone # to call after _____ weeks: _____

Or online at: _____

MAIL ORDER

My mail order purchase was for:

_____

The cost was $_____ and the order was

received on _____

Purchase Date: _____ Date Sent: _____

My Rebate/Mail Order was sent to:

Name _____

Address _____

City _____ State _____

                Zip Code _____

REBATE

I should be receiving $_____ for buying:

_____

I received my rebate on: _____

Phone # to call after _____ weeks: _____

Or online at: _____

MAIL ORDER

My mail order purchase was for:

_____

The cost was $_____ and the order was

received on _____

▪▪▪▪▪▪▪▪▪▪▪▪▪▪▪▪▪▪▪▪▪▪▪▪▪▪▪▪▪▪▪▪▪▪▪▪▪▪

Purchase Date: _____ Date Sent _____

My Rebate/Mail Order was sent to:

Name _____

Address _____

City _____ State _____

                Zip Code _____

REBATE

I should be receiving $_____ for buying:

_____

I received my rebate on: _____

Phone # to call after _____ weeks: _____

Or online at: _____

MAIL ORDER

My mail order purchase was for:

_____

The cost was $_____ and the order was

received on _____

Purchase Date: _____ Date Sent: _____
My Rebate/Mail Order was sent to:
Name _____
Address _____
City _____ State _____
                    Zip Code _____
REBATE
I should be receiving $_____ for buying:

_____
I received my rebate on: _____
Phone # to call after _____ weeks: _____
Or online at: _____
MAIL ORDER
My mail order purchase was for:

_____
The cost was $_____ and the order was
received on _____

Purchase Date: _____ Date Sent _____
My Rebate/Mail Order was sent to:
Name _____
Address _____
City _____ State _____
                    Zip Code _____
REBATE
I should be receiving $_____ for buying:

_____
I received my rebate on: _____
Phone # to call after _____ weeks: _____
Or online at: _____
MAIL ORDER
My mail order purchase was for:

_____
The cost was $_____ and the order was
received on _____

Purchase Date: _____ Date Sent: _____
My Rebate/Mail Order was sent to:
Name _____
Address _____
City _____ State _____
Zip Code _____

REBATE
I should be receiving $ _____ for buying:

_____
I received my rebate on: _____
Phone # to call after _____ weeks: _____
Or online at: _____
MAIL ORDER
My mail order purchase was for:

_____
The cost was $ _____ and the order was
received on _____

▪▪

Purchase Date: _____ Date Sent _____
My Rebate/Mail Order was sent to:
Name _____
Address _____
City _____ State _____
Zip Code _____

REBATE
I should be receiving $ _____ for buying:

_____
I received my rebate on: _____
Phone # to call after _____ weeks: _____
Or online at: _____
MAIL ORDER
My mail order purchase was for:

_____
The cost was $ _____ and the order was
received on _____

Purchase Date: _____ Date Sent: _____

My Rebate/Mail Order was sent to:

Name _____

Address _____

City _____ State _____

Zip Code _____

REBATE

I should be receiving $_____ for buying:

_____

I received my rebate on: _____

Phone # to call after _____ weeks: _____

Or online at: _____

MAIL ORDER

My mail order purchase was for:

_____

The cost was $_____ and the order was

received on _____

■▪■▪■▪■▪■▪■▪■▪■▪■▪■▪■▪■▪■▪■▪■▪■▪■▪■▪■▪■

Purchase Date: _____ Date Sent _____

My Rebate/Mail Order was sent to:

Name _____

Address _____

City _____ State _____

Zip Code _____

REBATE

I should be receiving $_____ for buying:

_____

I received my rebate on: _____

Phone # to call after _____ weeks: _____

Or online at: _____

MAIL ORDER

My mail order purchase was for:

_____

The cost was $_____ and the order was

received on _____

Purchase Date: _____ Date Sent: _____
My Rebate/Mail Order was sent to:
Name _____
Address _____
City _____ State _____
                    Zip Code _____

REBATE
I should be receiving $_____ for buying:

_____
I received my rebate on: _____
Phone # to call after _____ weeks: _____
Or online at: _____
MAIL ORDER
My mail order purchase was for:

_____
The cost was $_____ and the order was
received on _____

■■■■■■■■■■■■■■■■■■■■■■■■■■■■■■■■■■■■■■

Purchase Date: _____ Date Sent _____
My Rebate/Mail Order was sent to:
Name _____
Address _____
City _____ State _____
                    Zip Code _____

REBATE
I should be receiving $_____ for buying:

_____
I received my rebate on: _____
Phone # to call after _____ weeks: _____
Or online at: _____
MAIL ORDER
My mail order purchase was for:

_____
The cost was $_____ and the order was
received on _____

Purchase Date: _____ Date Sent: _____

My Rebate/Mail Order was sent to:

Name _____

Address _____

City _____ State _____

Zip Code _____

REBATE

I should be receiving $_____ for buying:

_____

I received my rebate on: _____

Phone # to call after _____ weeks: _____

Or online at: _____

MAIL ORDER

My mail order purchase was for:

_____

The cost was $_____ and the order was

received on _____

■■■■■■■■■■■■■■■■■■■■■■■■■■■■■■■■■■■■

Purchase Date: _____ Date Sent _____

My Rebate/Mail Order was sent to:

Name _____

Address _____

City _____ State _____

Zip Code _____

REBATE

I should be receiving $_____ for buying:

_____

I received my rebate on: _____

Phone # to call after _____ weeks: _____

Or online at: _____

MAIL ORDER

My mail order purchase was for:

_____

The cost was $_____ and the order was

received on _____

Purchase Date: _____ Date Sent: _____
My Rebate/Mail Order was sent to:
Name _____
Address _____
City _____ State _____
Zip Code _____

REBATE
I should be receiving $_____ for buying:

_____
I received my rebate on: _____
Phone # to call after _____ weeks: _____
Or online at: _____
MAIL ORDER
My mail order purchase was for:

_____
The cost was $_____ and the order was
received on _____

■■■■■■■■■■■■■■■■■■■■■■■■■■■■■■■■■■■■

Purchase Date: _____ Date Sent _____
My Rebate/Mail Order was sent to:
Name _____
Address _____
City _____ State _____
Zip Code _____

REBATE
I should be receiving $_____ for buying:

_____
I received my rebate on: _____
Phone # to call after _____ weeks: _____
Or online at: _____
MAIL ORDER
My mail order purchase was for:

_____
The cost was $_____ and the order was
received on _____

Purchase Date: _____ Date Sent: _____

My Rebate/Mail Order was sent to:

Name _____

Address _____

City _____ State _____

Zip Code _____

REBATE

I should be receiving $_____ for buying:

_____

I received my rebate on: _____

Phone # to call after _____ weeks: _____

Or online at: _____

MAIL ORDER

My mail order purchase was for:

_____

The cost was $_____ and the order was

received on _____

■■■■■■■■■■■■■■■■■■■■■■■■■■■■■■■■■■■■■■

Purchase Date: _____ Date Sent _____

My Rebate/Mail Order was sent to:

Name _____

Address _____

City _____ State _____

Zip Code _____

REBATE

I should be receiving $_____ for buying:

_____

I received my rebate on: _____

Phone # to call after _____ weeks: _____

Or online at: _____

MAIL ORDER

My mail order purchase was for:

_____

The cost was $_____ and the order was

received on _____

Purchase Date: _____ Date Sent: _____

My Rebate/Mail Order was sent to:

Name _____

Address _____

City _____ State _____

Zip Code _____

REBATE

I should be receiving $ _____ for buying:

_____

I received my rebate on: _____

Phone # to call after _____ weeks: _____

Or online at: _____

MAIL ORDER

My mail order purchase was for:

_____

The cost was $ _____ and the order was

received on _____

■■■■■■■■■■■■■■■■■■■■■■■■■■■■■■■■■■■■

Purchase Date: _____ Date Sent _____

My Rebate/Mail Order was sent to:

Name _____

Address _____

City _____ State _____

Zip Code _____

REBATE

I should be receiving $ _____ for buying:

_____

I received my rebate on: _____

Phone # to call after _____ weeks: _____

Or online at: _____

MAIL ORDER

My mail order purchase was for:

_____

The cost was $ _____ and the order was

received on _____

Purchase Date: _____ Date Sent: _____

My Rebate/Mail Order was sent to:

Name _____

Address _____

City _____ State _____

Zip Code _____

REBATE

I should be receiving $_____ for buying:

_____

I received my rebate on: _____

Phone # to call after _____ weeks: _____

Or online at: _____

MAIL ORDER

My mail order purchase was for:

_____

The cost was $_____ and the order was

received on _____

■■

Purchase Date: _____ Date Sent _____

My Rebate/Mail Order was sent to:

Name _____

Address _____

City _____ State _____

Zip Code _____

REBATE

I should be receiving $_____ for buying:

_____

I received my rebate on: _____

Phone # to call after _____ weeks: _____

Or online at: _____

MAIL ORDER

My mail order purchase was for:

_____

The cost was $_____ and the order was

received on _____

Purchase Date: _____ Date Sent: _____

My Rebate/Mail Order was sent to:

Name _____

Address _____

City _____ State _____

Zip Code _____

REBATE

I should be receiving $ _____ for buying:

_____

I received my rebate on: _____

Phone # to call after _____ weeks: _____

Or online at: _____

MAIL ORDER

My mail order purchase was for:

_____

The cost was $ _____ and the order was

received on _____

Purchase Date: _____ Date Sent _____

My Rebate/Mail Order was sent to:

Name _____

Address _____

City _____ State _____

Zip Code _____

REBATE

I should be receiving $ _____ for buying:

_____

I received my rebate on: _____

Phone # to call after _____ weeks: _____

Or online at: _____

MAIL ORDER

My mail order purchase was for:

_____

The cost was $ _____ and the order was

received on _____

Purchase Date: _____ Date Sent: _____

My Rebate/Mail Order was sent to:

Name _____

Address _____

City _____ State _____

Zip Code _____

REBATE

I should be receiving $ _____ for buying:

_____

I received my rebate on: _____

Phone # to call after _____ weeks: _____

Or online at: _____

MAIL ORDER

My mail order purchase was for:

_____

The cost was $ _____ and the order was

received on _____

■■

Purchase Date: _____ Date Sent _____

My Rebate/Mail Order was sent to:

Name _____

Address _____

City _____ State _____

Zip Code _____

REBATE

I should be receiving $ _____ for buying:

_____

I received my rebate on: _____

Phone # to call after _____ weeks: _____

Or online at: _____

MAIL ORDER

My mail order purchase was for:

_____

The cost was $ _____ and the order was

received on _____

Purchase Date: _____   Date Sent: _____
My Rebate/Mail Order was sent to:
Name _____
Address _____
City _____   State _____
                    Zip Code _____

REBATE
I should be receiving $ _____ for buying:

_____
I received my rebate on: _____
Phone # to call after _____ weeks: _____
Or online at: _____
MAIL ORDER
My mail order purchase was for:

_____
The cost was $ _____ and the order was
received on _____

▮▮▮▮▮▮▮▮▮▮▮▮▮▮▮▮▮▮▮▮▮▮▮▮▮▮▮▮▮▮▮▮▮

Purchase Date: _____   Date Sent _____
My Rebate/Mail Order was sent to:
Name _____
Address _____
City _____   State _____
                    Zip Code _____

REBATE
I should be receiving $ _____ for buying:

_____
I received my rebate on: _____
Phone # to call after _____ weeks: _____
Or online at: _____
MAIL ORDER
My mail order purchase was for:

_____
The cost was $ _____ and the order was
received on _____

Purchase Date: _____ Date Sent: _____

My Rebate/Mail Order was sent to:

Name _____

Address _____

City _____ State _____

Zip Code _____

REBATE

I should be receiving $ _____ for buying:

_____

I received my rebate on: _____

Phone # to call after _____ weeks: _____

Or online at: _____

MAIL ORDER

My mail order purchase was for:

_____

The cost was $ _____ and the order was

received on _____

■■■■■■■■■■■■■■■■■■■■■■■■■■■■■■■■■■■■■■■

Purchase Date: _____ Date Sent _____

My Rebate/Mail Order was sent to:

Name _____

Address _____

City _____ State _____

Zip Code _____

REBATE

I should be receiving $ _____ for buying:

_____

I received my rebate on: _____

Phone # to call after _____ weeks: _____

Or online at: _____

MAIL ORDER

My mail order purchase was for:

_____

The cost was $ _____ and the order was

received on _____

Purchase Date: _____ Date Sent: _____
My Rebate/Mail Order was sent to:
Name _____
Address _____
City _____ State _____
Zip Code _____

REBATE
I should be receiving $_____ for buying:

_____
I received my rebate on: _____
Phone # to call after _____ weeks: _____
Or online at: _____
MAIL ORDER
My mail order purchase was for:

_____
The cost was $_____ and the order was
received on _____

▪▪▪▪▪▪▪▪▪▪▪▪▪▪▪▪▪▪▪▪▪▪▪▪▪▪▪▪▪▪▪▪

Purchase Date: _____ Date Sent _____
My Rebate/Mail Order was sent to:
Name _____
Address _____
City _____ State _____
Zip Code _____

REBATE
I should be receiving $_____ for buying:

_____
I received my rebate on: _____
Phone # to call after _____ weeks: _____
Or online at: _____
MAIL ORDER
My mail order purchase was for:

_____
The cost was $_____ and the order was
received on _____

Purchase Date: _____ Date Sent: _____

My Rebate/Mail Order was sent to:

Name _____

Address _____

City _____ State _____

Zip Code _____

REBATE

I should be receiving $_____ for buying:

_____

I received my rebate on: _____

Phone # to call after _____ weeks: _____

Or online at: _____

MAIL ORDER

My mail order purchase was for:

_____

The cost was $_____ and the order was

received on _____

▪▪▪▪▪▪▪▪▪▪▪▪▪▪▪▪▪▪▪▪▪▪▪▪▪▪▪▪▪▪▪▪▪▪▪▪▪▪▪

Purchase Date: _____ Date Sent _____

My Rebate/Mail Order was sent to:

Name _____

Address _____

City _____ State _____

Zip Code _____

REBATE

I should be receiving $_____ for buying:

_____

I received my rebate on: _____

Phone # to call after _____ weeks: _____

Or online at: _____

MAIL ORDER

My mail order purchase was for:

_____

The cost was $_____ and the order was

received on _____

Purchase Date: _____ Date Sent: _____
My Rebate/Mail Order was sent to:
Name _____
Address _____
City _____ State _____
                        Zip Code _____
REBATE
I should be receiving $ _____ for buying:

_____
I received my rebate on: _____
Phone # to call after _____ weeks: _____
Or online at: _____
MAIL ORDER
My mail order purchase was for:

_____
The cost was $ _____ and the order was
received on _____

██

Purchase Date: _____ Date Sent _____
My Rebate/Mail Order was sent to:
Name _____
Address _____
City _____ State _____
                        Zip Code _____
REBATE
I should be receiving $ _____ for buying:

_____
I received my rebate on: _____
Phone # to call after _____ weeks: _____
Or online at: _____
MAIL ORDER
My mail order purchase was for:

_____
The cost was $ _____ and the order was
received on _____

Purchase Date: _____ Date Sent: _____

My Rebate/Mail Order was sent to:

Name _____

Address _____

City _____ State _____

Zip Code _____

REBATE

I should be receiving $_____ for buying:

_____

I received my rebate on: _____

Phone # to call after _____ weeks: _____

Or online at: _____

MAIL ORDER

My mail order purchase was for:

_____

The cost was $_____ and the order was received on _____

■■

Purchase Date: _____ Date Sent _____

My Rebate/Mail Order was sent to:

Name _____

Address _____

City _____ State _____

Zip Code _____

REBATE

I should be receiving $_____ for buying:

_____

I received my rebate on: _____

Phone # to call after _____ weeks: _____

Or online at: _____

MAIL ORDER

My mail order purchase was for:

_____

The cost was $_____ and the order was received on _____

Purchase Date: _____ Date Sent: _____
My Rebate/Mail Order was sent to:
Name _____
Address _____
City _____ State _____
Zip Code _____

REBATE
I should be receiving $_____ for buying:

_____
I received my rebate on: _____
Phone # to call after _____ weeks: _____
Or online at: _____
MAIL ORDER
My mail order purchase was for:

_____
The cost was $_____ and the order was
received on _____

▪▪▪▪▪▪▪▪▪▪▪▪▪▪▪▪▪▪▪▪▪▪▪▪▪▪▪▪▪▪▪▪▪▪▪▪▪▪

Purchase Date: _____ Date Sent _____
My Rebate/Mail Order was sent to:
Name _____
Address _____
City _____ State _____
Zip Code _____

REBATE
I should be receiving $_____ for buying:

_____
I received my rebate on: _____
Phone # to call after _____ weeks: _____
Or online at: _____
MAIL ORDER
My mail order purchase was for:

_____
The cost was $_____ and the order was
received on _____

Purchase Date: _____ Date Sent: _____
My Rebate/Mail Order was sent to:
Name _____
Address _____
City _____ State _____
                    Zip Code _____
REBATE
I should be receiving $_____ for buying:
_____
I received my rebate on: _____
Phone # to call after _____ weeks: _____
Or online at: _____
MAIL ORDER
My mail order purchase was for:
_____
The cost was $_____ and the order was
received on _____

■■■

Purchase Date: _____ Date Sent _____
My Rebate/Mail Order was sent to:
Name _____
Address _____
City _____ State _____
                    Zip Code _____
REBATE
I should be receiving $_____ for buying:
_____
I received my rebate on: _____
Phone # to call after _____ weeks: _____
Or online at: _____
MAIL ORDER
My mail order purchase was for:
_____
The cost was $_____ and the order was
received on _____

Purchase Date: _____ Date Sent: _____

My Rebate/Mail Order was sent to:

Name _____

Address _____

City _____ State _____

Zip Code _____

REBATE

I should be receiving $_____ for buying:

_____

I received my rebate on: _____

Phone # to call after _____ weeks: _____

Or online at: _____

MAIL ORDER

My mail order purchase was for:

_____

The cost was $_____ and the order was

received on _____

■■

Purchase Date: _____ Date Sent _____

My Rebate/Mail Order was sent to:

Name _____

Address _____

City _____ State _____

Zip Code _____

REBATE

I should be receiving $_____ for buying:

_____

I received my rebate on: _____

Phone # to call after _____ weeks: _____

Or online at: _____

MAIL ORDER

My mail order purchase was for:

_____

The cost was $_____ and the order was

received on _____

Purchase Date: _____ Date Sent: _____
My Rebate/Mail Order was sent to:
Name _____
Address _____
City _____ State _____
                     Zip Code _____

REBATE
I should be receiving $_____ for buying:

_____
I received my rebate on: _____
Phone # to call after _____ weeks: _____
Or online at: _____
MAIL ORDER
My mail order purchase was for:

_____
The cost was $_____ and the order was
received on _____

━━━━━━━━━━━━━━━━━━━━━━━━━━━━━━

Purchase Date: _____ Date Sent _____
My Rebate/Mail Order was sent to:
Name _____
Address _____
City _____ State _____
                     Zip Code _____

REBATE
I should be receiving $_____ for buying:

_____
I received my rebate on: _____
Phone # to call after _____ weeks: _____
Or online at: _____
MAIL ORDER
My mail order purchase was for:

_____
The cost was $_____ and the order was
received on _____

Purchase Date: _____ Date Sent: _____

My Rebate/Mail Order was sent to:

Name _____

Address _____

City _____ State _____

Zip Code _____

REBATE

I should be receiving $ _____ for buying:

_____

I received my rebate on: _____

Phone # to call after _____ weeks: _____

Or online at: _____

MAIL ORDER

My mail order purchase was for:

_____

The cost was $ _____ and the order was

received on _____

■■

Purchase Date: _____ Date Sent _____

My Rebate/Mail Order was sent to:

Name _____

Address _____

City _____ State _____

Zip Code _____

REBATE

I should be receiving $ _____ for buying:

_____

I received my rebate on: _____

Phone # to call after _____ weeks: _____

Or online at: _____

MAIL ORDER

My mail order purchase was for:

_____

The cost was $ _____ and the order was

received on _____

Purchase Date: _____ Date Sent: _____

My Rebate/Mail Order was sent to:

Name _____

Address _____

City _____ State _____

Zip Code _____

REBATE

I should be receiving $_____ for buying:

_____

I received my rebate on: _____

Phone # to call after _____ weeks: _____

Or online at: _____

MAIL ORDER

My mail order purchase was for:

_____

The cost was $_____ and the order was

received on _____

■■■■■■■■■■■■■■■■■■■■■■■■■■■■■■■■■■■■■

Purchase Date: _____ Date Sent _____

My Rebate/Mail Order was sent to:

Name _____

Address _____

City _____ State _____

Zip Code _____

REBATE

I should be receiving $_____ for buying:

_____

I received my rebate on: _____

Phone # to call after _____ weeks: _____

Or online at: _____

MAIL ORDER

My mail order purchase was for:

_____

The cost was $_____ and the order was

received on _____

Purchase Date: _____ Date Sent: _____

My Rebate/Mail Order was sent to:

Name _____

Address _____

City _____ State _____

Zip Code _____

REBATE

I should be receiving $_____ for buying:

_____

I received my rebate on: _____

Phone # to call after _____ weeks: _____

Or online at: _____

MAIL ORDER

My mail order purchase was for:

_____

The cost was $_____ and the order was

received on _____

■■

Purchase Date: _____ Date Sent _____

My Rebate/Mail Order was sent to:

Name _____

Address _____

City _____ State _____

Zip Code _____

REBATE

I should be receiving $_____ for buying:

_____

I received my rebate on: _____

Phone # to call after _____ weeks: _____

Or online at: _____

MAIL ORDER

My mail order purchase was for:

_____

The cost was $_____ and the order was

received on _____

Purchase Date: _____ Date Sent: _____
My Rebate/Mail Order was sent to:
Name _____
Address _____
City _____ State _____
Zip Code _____

REBATE
I should be receiving $_____ for buying:
_____
I received my rebate on: _____
Phone # to call after _____ weeks: _____
Or online at: _____
MAIL ORDER
My mail order purchase was for:
_____
The cost was $_____ and the order was
received on _____

■■■■■■■■■■■■■■■■■■■■■■■■■■■■■■■■■■■■■■■

Purchase Date: _____ Date Sent _____
My Rebate/Mail Order was sent to:
Name _____
Address _____
City _____ State _____
Zip Code _____

REBATE
I should be receiving $_____ for buying:
_____
I received my rebate on: _____
Phone # to call after _____ weeks: _____
Or online at: _____
MAIL ORDER
My mail order purchase was for:
_____
The cost was $_____ and the order was
received on _____

94

Purchase Date: _____ Date Sent: _____

My Rebate/Mail Order was sent to:

Name _____

Address _____

City _____ State _____

Zip Code _____

REBATE

I should be receiving $_____ for buying:

_____

I received my rebate on: _____

Phone # to call after _____ weeks: _____

Or online at: _____

MAIL ORDER

My mail order purchase was for:

_____

The cost was $_____ and the order was

received on _____

■■

Purchase Date: _____ Date Sent _____

My Rebate/Mail Order was sent to:

Name _____

Address _____

City _____ State _____

Zip Code _____

REBATE

I should be receiving $_____ for buying:

_____

I received my rebate on: _____

Phone # to call after _____ weeks: _____

Or online at: _____

MAIL ORDER

My mail order purchase was for:

_____

The cost was $_____ and the order was

received on _____

Purchase Date: _____ Date Sent: _____

My Rebate/Mail Order was sent to:

Name _____

Address _____

City _____ State _____

Zip Code _____

REBATE

I should be receiving $_____ for buying:

_____

I received my rebate on: _____

Phone # to call after _____ weeks: _____

Or online at: _____

MAIL ORDER

My mail order purchase was for:

_____

The cost was $_____ and the order was

received on _____

■■■■■■■■■■■■■■■■■■■■■■■■■■■■■■■■■■■

Purchase Date: _____ Date Sent _____

My Rebate/Mail Order was sent to:

Name _____

Address _____

City _____ State _____

Zip Code _____

REBATE

I should be receiving $_____ for buying:

_____

I received my rebate on: _____

Phone # to call after _____ weeks: _____

Or online at: _____

MAIL ORDER

My mail order purchase was for:

_____

The cost was $_____ and the order was

received on _____

Purchase Date: _____ Date Sent: _____
My Rebate/Mail Order was sent to:
Name _____
Address _____
City _____ State _____
Zip Code _____

REBATE
I should be receiving $_____ for buying:

_____
I received my rebate on: _____
Phone # to call after _____ weeks: _____
Or online at: _____
MAIL ORDER
My mail order purchase was for:

_____
The cost was $_____ and the order was
received on _____

■■■

Purchase Date: _____ Date Sent _____
My Rebate/Mail Order was sent to:
Name _____
Address _____
City _____ State _____
Zip Code _____

REBATE
I should be receiving $_____ for buying:

_____
I received my rebate on: _____
Phone # to call after _____ weeks: _____
Or online at: _____
MAIL ORDER
My mail order purchase was for:

_____
The cost was $_____ and the order was
received on _____

Purchase Date: _____ Date Sent: _____
My Rebate/Mail Order was sent to:
Name _____
Address _____
City _____ State _____
Zip Code _____

REBATE
I should be receiving $_____ for buying:

_____
I received my rebate on: _____
 Phone # to call after _____ weeks: _____
Or online at: _____
MAIL ORDER
My mail order purchase was for:

_____
The cost was $_____ and the order was
received on _____

■■■■■■■■■■■■■■■■■■■■■■■■■■■■■■■■■■■■■■

Purchase Date: _____ Date Sent _____
My Rebate/Mail Order was sent to:
Name _____
Address _____
City _____ State _____
Zip Code _____

REBATE
I should be receiving $_____ for buying:

_____
I received my rebate on: _____
 Phone # to call after _____ weeks: _____
Or online at: _____
MAIL ORDER
My mail order purchase was for:

_____
The cost was $_____ and the order was
received on _____

Purchase Date: _____ Date Sent: _____
My Rebate/Mail Order was sent to:
Name _____
Address _____
City _____ State _____
　　　　　　Zip Code _____

REBATE
I should be receiving $_____ for buying:
_____
I received my rebate on: _____
Phone # to call after _____ weeks: _____
Or online at: _____
MAIL ORDER
My mail order purchase was for:
_____
The cost was $_____ and the order was
received on _____

▮▮▮▮▮▮▮▮▮▮▮▮▮▮▮▮▮▮▮▮▮▮▮▮▮▮▮▮▮▮▮▮▮▮▮▮▮▮▮

Purchase Date: _____ Date Sent _____
My Rebate/Mail Order was sent to:
Name _____
Address _____
City _____ State _____
　　　　　　Zip Code _____

REBATE
I should be receiving $_____ for buying:
_____
I received my rebate on: _____
Phone # to call after _____ weeks: _____
Or online at: _____
MAIL ORDER
My mail order purchase was for:
_____
The cost was $_____ and the order was
received on _____

Purchase Date: _____ Date Sent: _____

My Rebate/Mail Order was sent to:

Name _____

Address _____

City _____ State _____

Zip Code _____

REBATE

I should be receiving $ _____ for buying:

_____

I received my rebate on: _____

Phone # to call after _____ weeks: _____

Or online at: _____

MAIL ORDER

My mail order purchase was for:

_____

The cost was $ _____ and the order was

received on _____

■■■

Purchase Date: _____ Date Sent _____

My Rebate/Mail Order was sent to:

Name _____

Address _____

City _____ State _____

Zip Code _____

REBATE

I should be receiving $ _____ for buying:

_____

I received my rebate on: _____

Phone # to call after _____ weeks: _____

Or online at: _____

MAIL ORDER

My mail order purchase was for:

_____

The cost was $ _____ and the order was

received on _____

Purchase Date: _____   Date Sent: _____

My Rebate/Mail Order was sent to:

Name _____

Address _____

City _____   State _____

Zip Code _____

REBATE

I should be receiving $_____   for buying:

_____

I received my rebate on: _____

Phone # to call after _____ weeks: _____

Or online at: _____

MAIL ORDER

My mail order purchase was for:

_____

The cost was $_____   and the order was

received on   _____

Purchase Date: _____   Date Sent _____

My Rebate/Mail Order was sent to:

Name _____

Address _____

City _____   State _____

Zip Code _____

REBATE

I should be receiving $_____   for buying:

_____

I received my rebate on: _____

Phone # to call after _____ weeks: _____

Or online at: _____

MAIL ORDER

My mail order purchase was for:

_____

The cost was $_____   and the order was

received on   _____

Purchase Date: _____ Date Sent: _____
My Rebate/Mail Order was sent to:
Name _____
Address _____
City _____ State _____
                    Zip Code _____
REBATE
I should be receiving $_____ for buying:

_____
I received my rebate on: _____
 Phone # to call after _____ weeks: _____
Or online at: _____
MAIL ORDER
My mail order purchase was for:

_____
The cost was $_____ and the order was
received on _____

▪▪▪▪▪▪▪▪▪▪▪▪▪▪▪▪▪▪▪▪▪▪▪▪▪▪▪▪▪▪▪▪▪▪▪▪▪

Purchase Date: _____ Date Sent _____
My Rebate/Mail Order was sent to:
Name _____
Address _____
City _____ State _____
                    Zip Code _____
REBATE
I should be receiving $_____ for buying:

_____
I received my rebate on: _____
 Phone # to call after _____ weeks: _____
Or online at: _____
MAIL ORDER
My mail order purchase was for:

_____
The cost was $_____ and the order was
received on _____

Purchase Date: _____ Date Sent: _____
My Rebate/Mail Order was sent to:
Name _____
Address _____
City _____ State _____
                    Zip Code _____

REBATE
I should be receiving $_____ for buying:

_____
I received my rebate on: _____
Phone # to call after _____ weeks: _____
Or online at: _____
MAIL ORDER
My mail order purchase was for:

_____
The cost was $_____ and the order was
received on _____

■■

Purchase Date: _____ Date Sent _____
My Rebate/Mail Order was sent to:
Name _____
Address _____
City _____ State _____
                    Zip Code _____

REBATE
I should be receiving $_____ for buying:

_____
I received my rebate on: _____
Phone # to call after _____ weeks: _____
Or online at: _____
MAIL ORDER
My mail order purchase was for:

_____
The cost was $_____ and the order was
received on _____

Purchase Date: _____ Date Sent: _____

My Rebate/Mail Order was sent to:

Name _____

Address _____

City _____ State _____

Zip Code _____

REBATE

I should be receiving $_____ for buying:

_____

I received my rebate on: _____

 Phone # to call after _____ weeks: _____

Or online at: _____

MAIL ORDER

My mail order purchase was for:

_____

The cost was $_____ and the order was

received on _____

■▪■▪■▪■▪■▪■▪■▪■▪■▪■▪■▪■▪■▪■▪■▪■▪■▪■▪■

Purchase Date: _____ Date Sent _____

My Rebate/Mail Order was sent to:

Name _____

Address _____

City _____ State _____

Zip Code _____

REBATE

I should be receiving $_____ for buying:

_____

I received my rebate on: _____

 Phone # to call after _____ weeks: _____

Or online at: _____

MAIL ORDER

My mail order purchase was for:

_____

The cost was $_____ and the order was

received on _____

Purchase Date: _____ Date Sent: _____
My Rebate/Mail Order was sent to:
Name _____
Address _____
City _____ State _____
              Zip Code _____

REBATE
I should be receiving $_____ for buying:
_____
I received my rebate on: _____
Phone # to call after _____ weeks: _____
Or online at: _____
MAIL ORDER
My mail order purchase was for:
_____
The cost was $_____ and the order was
received on _____

▪▪

Purchase Date: _____ Date Sent _____
My Rebate/Mail Order was sent to:
Name _____
Address _____
City _____ State _____
              Zip Code _____

REBATE
I should be receiving $_____ for buying:
_____
I received my rebate on: _____
Phone # to call after _____ weeks: _____
Or online at: _____
MAIL ORDER
My mail order purchase was for:
_____
The cost was $_____ and the order was
received on _____

Purchase Date: _____ Date Sent: _____
My Rebate/Mail Order was sent to:
Name _____
Address _____
City _____ State _____
Zip Code _____

REBATE

I should be receiving $_____ for buying:

_____
I received my rebate on: _____
Phone # to call after _____ weeks: _____
Or online at: _____
MAIL ORDER
My mail order purchase was for:

_____
The cost was $_____ and the order was
received on _____

■■■■■■■■■■■■■■■■■■■■■■■■■■■■■■■■■

Purchase Date: _____ Date Sent _____
My Rebate/Mail Order was sent to:
Name _____
Address _____
City _____ State _____
Zip Code _____

REBATE

I should be receiving $_____ for buying:

_____
I received my rebate on: _____
Phone # to call after _____ weeks: _____
Or online at: _____
MAIL ORDER
My mail order purchase was for:

_____
The cost was $_____ and the order was
received on _____

Purchase Date: _____ Date Sent: _____
My Rebate/Mail Order was sent to:
Name _____
Address _____
City _____ State _____
Zip Code _____

REBATE
I should be receiving $_____ for buying:

_____
I received my rebate on: _____
Phone # to call after _____ weeks: _____
Or online at: _____
MAIL ORDER
My mail order purchase was for:

_____
The cost was $_____ and the order was
received on _____

Purchase Date: _____ Date Sent _____
My Rebate/Mail Order was sent to:
Name _____
Address _____
City _____ State _____
Zip Code _____

REBATE
I should be receiving $_____ for buying:

_____
I received my rebate on: _____
Phone # to call after _____ weeks: _____
Or online at: _____
MAIL ORDER
My mail order purchase was for:

_____
The cost was $_____ and the order was
received on _____

Purchase Date: _____ Date Sent: _____
My Rebate/Mail Order was sent to:
Name _____
Address _____
City _____ State _____
                    Zip Code _____
REBATE
I should be receiving $ _____ for buying:

_____
I received my rebate on: _____
 Phone # to call after _____ weeks: _____
Or online at: _____
MAIL ORDER
My mail order purchase was for:

_____
The cost was $ _____ and the order was
received on _____

■·■

Purchase Date: _____ Date Sent _____
My Rebate/Mail Order was sent to:
Name _____
Address _____
City _____ State _____
                    Zip Code _____
REBATE
I should be receiving $ _____ for buying:

_____
I received my rebate on: _____
 Phone # to call after _____ weeks: _____
Or online at: _____
MAIL ORDER
My mail order purchase was for:

_____
The cost was $ _____ and the order was
received on _____

Purchase Date: _____ Date Sent: _____

My Rebate/Mail Order was sent to:

Name _____

Address _____

City _____ State _____

Zip Code _____

REBATE

I should be receiving $_____ for buying:

_____

I received my rebate on: _____

Phone # to call after _____ weeks: _____

Or online at: _____

MAIL ORDER

My mail order purchase was for:

_____

The cost was $_____ and the order was

received on _____

■■

Purchase Date: _____ Date Sent _____

My Rebate/Mail Order was sent to:

Name _____

Address _____

City _____ State _____

Zip Code _____

REBATE

I should be receiving $_____ for buying:

_____

I received my rebate on: _____

Phone # to call after _____ weeks: _____

Or online at: _____

MAIL ORDER

My mail order purchase was for:

_____

The cost was $_____ and the order was

received on _____

Purchase Date: _____ Date Sent: _____
My Rebate/Mail Order was sent to:
Name _____
Address _____
City _____ State _____
                    Zip Code _____
REBATE
I should be receiving $_____ for buying:

_____
I received my rebate on: _____
 Phone # to call after _____ weeks: _____
Or online at: _____
MAIL ORDER
My mail order purchase was for:

_____
The cost was $_____ and the order was
received on   _____

▪▪▪▪▪▪▪▪▪▪▪▪▪▪▪▪▪▪▪▪▪▪▪▪▪▪▪▪▪▪▪▪▪▪▪▪▪▪

Purchase Date: _____ Date Sent _____
My Rebate/Mail Order was sent to:
Name _____
Address _____
City _____ State _____
                    Zip Code _____
REBATE
I should be receiving $_____ for buying:

_____
I received my rebate on: _____
 Phone # to call after _____ weeks: _____
Or online at: _____
MAIL ORDER
My mail order purchase was for:

_____
The cost was $_____ and the order was
received on   _____

Purchase Date: _____ Date Sent: _____
My Rebate/Mail Order was sent to:
Name _____
Address _____
City _____ State _____
Zip Code _____

REBATE
I should be receiving $ _____ for buying:

_____
I received my rebate on: _____
Phone # to call after _____ weeks: _____
Or online at: _____
MAIL ORDER
My mail order purchase was for:

_____
The cost was $ _____ and the order was
received on _____

▪▪▪▪▪▪▪▪▪▪▪▪▪▪▪▪▪▪▪▪▪▪▪▪▪▪▪▪▪▪▪▪▪▪▪▪▪▪

Purchase Date: _____ Date Sent _____
My Rebate/Mail Order was sent to:
Name _____
Address _____
City _____ State _____
Zip Code _____

REBATE
I should be receiving $ _____ for buying:

_____
I received my rebate on: _____
Phone # to call after _____ weeks: _____
Or online at: _____
MAIL ORDER
My mail order purchase was for:

_____
The cost was $ _____ and the order was
received on _____

Purchase Date: _____ Date Sent: _____
My Rebate/Mail Order was sent to:
Name _____
Address _____
City _____ State _____
              Zip Code _____
REBATE
I should be receiving $_____ for buying:

_____
I received my rebate on: _____
Phone # to call after _____ weeks: _____
Or online at: _____
MAIL ORDER
My mail order purchase was for:

_____
The cost was $_____ and the order was
received on _____

Purchase Date: _____ Date Sent _____
My Rebate/Mail Order was sent to:
Name _____
Address _____
City _____ State _____
              Zip Code _____
REBATE
I should be receiving $_____ for buying:

_____
I received my rebate on: _____
Phone # to call after _____ weeks: _____
Or online at: _____
MAIL ORDER
My mail order purchase was for:

_____
The cost was $_____ and the order was
received on _____

Purchase Date: _____ Date Sent: _____

My Rebate/Mail Order was sent to:

Name _____

Address _____

City _____ State _____

Zip Code _____

REBATE

I should be receiving $_____ for buying:

_____

I received my rebate on: _____

Phone # to call after _____ weeks: _____

Or online at: _____

MAIL ORDER

My mail order purchase was for:

_____

The cost was $_____ and the order was

received on _____

■■■■■■■■■■■■■■■■■■■■■■■■■■■■■■■■■■■■

Purchase Date: _____ Date Sent _____

My Rebate/Mail Order was sent to:

Name _____

Address _____

City _____ State _____

Zip Code _____

REBATE

I should be receiving $_____ for buying:

_____

I received my rebate on: _____

Phone # to call after _____ weeks: _____

Or online at: _____

MAIL ORDER

My mail order purchase was for:

_____

The cost was $_____ and the order was

received on _____

Purchase Date: _____ Date Sent: _____
My Rebate/Mail Order was sent to:
Name _____
Address _____
City _____ State _____
Zip Code _____
REBATE
I should be receiving $ _____ for buying:
_____
I received my rebate on: _____
 Phone # to call after _____ weeks: _____
Or online at: _____
MAIL ORDER
My mail order purchase was for:
_____
The cost was $ _____ and the order was
received on _____

■■

Purchase Date: _____ Date Sent _____
My Rebate/Mail Order was sent to:
Name _____
Address _____
City _____ State _____
Zip Code _____
REBATE
I should be receiving $ _____ for buying:
_____
I received my rebate on: _____
 Phone # to call after _____ weeks: _____
Or online at: _____
MAIL ORDER
My mail order purchase was for:
_____
The cost was $ _____ and the order was
received on _____

Purchase Date: _____ Date Sent: _____
My Rebate/Mail Order was sent to:
Name _____
Address _____
City _____ State _____
                       Zip Code _____

REBATE
I should be receiving $ _____ for buying:
_____
I received my rebate on: _____
Phone # to call after _____ weeks: _____
Or online at: _____
MAIL ORDER
My mail order purchase was for:
_____
The cost was $ _____ and the order was
received on _____

▪▪▪▪▪▪▪▪▪▪▪▪▪▪▪▪▪▪▪▪▪▪▪▪▪▪▪▪▪▪▪▪▪▪▪▪

Purchase Date: _____ Date Sent _____
My Rebate/Mail Order was sent to:
Name _____
Address _____
City _____ State _____
                       Zip Code _____

REBATE
I should be receiving $ _____ for buying:
_____
I received my rebate on: _____
Phone # to call after _____ weeks: _____
Or online at: _____
MAIL ORDER
My mail order purchase was for:
_____
The cost was $ _____ and the order was
received on _____

Purchase Date: _____ Date Sent: _____
My Rebate/Mail Order was sent to:
Name _____
Address _____
City _____ State _____
                    Zip Code _____
REBATE
I should be receiving $_____ for buying:

_____
I received my rebate on: _____
 Phone # to call after _____ weeks: _____
Or online at: _____
MAIL ORDER
My mail order purchase was for:

_____
The cost was $_____ and the order was
received on   _____

■■■■■■■■■■■■■■■■■■■■■■■■■■■■■■■■■■■■■■■

Purchase Date: _____ Date Sent _____
My Rebate/Mail Order was sent to:
Name _____
Address _____
City _____ State _____
                    Zip Code _____
REBATE
I should be receiving $_____ for buying:

_____
I received my rebate on: _____
 Phone # to call after _____ weeks: _____
Or online at: _____
MAIL ORDER
My mail order purchase was for:

_____
The cost was $_____ and the order was
received on   _____

Purchase Date: _____ Date Sent: _____
My Rebate/Mail Order was sent to:
Name _____
Address _____
City _____ State _____
Zip Code _____

REBATE
I should be receiving $_____ for buying:
_____
I received my rebate on: _____
Phone # to call after _____ weeks: _____
Or online at: _____
MAIL ORDER
My mail order purchase was for:
_____
The cost was $_____ and the order was
received on _____

▪▪▪▪▪▪▪▪▪▪▪▪▪▪▪▪▪▪▪▪▪▪▪▪▪▪▪▪▪▪▪▪▪▪▪▪

Purchase Date: _____ Date Sent _____
My Rebate/Mail Order was sent to:
Name _____
Address _____
City _____ State _____
Zip Code _____

REBATE
I should be receiving $_____ for buying:
_____
I received my rebate on: _____
Phone # to call after _____ weeks: _____
Or online at: _____
MAIL ORDER
My mail order purchase was for:
_____
The cost was $_____ and the order was
received on _____

Purchase Date: _____ Date Sent: _____
My Rebate/Mail Order was sent to:
Name _____
Address _____
City _____ State _____
Zip Code _____

REBATE
I should be receiving $_____ for buying:

I received my rebate on: _____
Phone # to call after _____ weeks: _____
Or online at: _____
MAIL ORDER
My mail order purchase was for:

The cost was $_____ and the order was
received on _____

■■■■■■■■■■■■■■■■■■■■■■■■■■■■■■■■■■■■■■■

Purchase Date: _____ Date Sent _____
My Rebate/Mail Order was sent to:
Name _____
Address _____
City _____ State _____
Zip Code _____

REBATE
I should be receiving $_____ for buying:

I received my rebate on: _____
Phone # to call after _____ weeks: _____
Or online at: _____
MAIL ORDER
My mail order purchase was for:

The cost was $_____ and the order was
received on _____

Purchase Date: _____ Date Sent: _____

My Rebate/Mail Order was sent to:

Name _____

Address _____

City _____ State _____

Zip Code _____

REBATE

I should be receiving $_____ for buying:

_____

I received my rebate on: _____

Phone # to call after _____ weeks: _____

Or online at: _____

MAIL ORDER

My mail order purchase was for:

_____

The cost was $_____ and the order was

received on _____

▪▪

Purchase Date: _____ Date Sent _____

My Rebate/Mail Order was sent to:

Name _____

Address _____

City _____ State _____

Zip Code _____

REBATE

I should be receiving $_____ for buying:

_____

I received my rebate on: _____

Phone # to call after _____ weeks: _____

Or online at: _____

MAIL ORDER

My mail order purchase was for:

_____

The cost was $_____ and the order was

received on _____

Purchase Date: _____ Date Sent: _____
My Rebate/Mail Order was sent to:
Name _____
Address _____
City _____ State _____
Zip Code _____
REBATE
I should be receiving $_____ for buying:

_____
I received my rebate on: _____
Phone # to call after _____ weeks: _____
Or online at: _____
MAIL ORDER
My mail order purchase was for:

_____
The cost was $_____ and the order was
received on _____

■·■■■■·■■·■■·■■·■■·■■·■■·■■·■■·■■■·■

Purchase Date: _____ Date Sent _____
My Rebate/Mail Order was sent to:
Name _____
Address _____
City _____ State _____
Zip Code _____
REBATE
I should be receiving $_____ for buying:

_____
I received my rebate on: _____
Phone # to call after _____ weeks: _____
Or online at: _____
MAIL ORDER
My mail order purchase was for:

_____
The cost was $_____ and the order was
received on _____

Purchase Date: _____ Date Sent: _____
My Rebate/Mail Order was sent to:
Name _____
Address _____
City _____ State _____
                    Zip Code _____

REBATE
I should be receiving $_____ for buying:

_____
I received my rebate on: _____
Phone # to call after _____ weeks: _____
Or online at: _____
MAIL ORDER
My mail order purchase was for:

_____
The cost was $_____ and the order was
received on _____

▪▪▪▪▪▪▪▪▪▪▪▪▪▪▪▪▪▪▪▪▪▪▪▪▪▪▪▪▪▪▪▪▪▪▪▪▪

Purchase Date: _____ Date Sent _____
My Rebate/Mail Order was sent to:
Name _____
Address _____
City _____ State _____
                    Zip Code _____

REBATE
I should be receiving $_____ for buying:

_____
I received my rebate on: _____
Phone # to call after _____ weeks: _____
Or online at: _____
MAIL ORDER
My mail order purchase was for:

_____
The cost was $_____ and the order was
received on _____

Purchase Date: _____ Date Sent: _____

My Rebate/Mail Order was sent to:

Name _____

Address _____

City _____ State _____

Zip Code _____

REBATE

I should be receiving $ _____ for buying:

_____

I received my rebate on: _____

Phone # to call after _____ weeks: _____

Or online at: _____

MAIL ORDER

My mail order purchase was for:

_____

The cost was $ _____ and the order was

received on _____

■■■

Purchase Date: _____ Date Sent _____

My Rebate/Mail Order was sent to:

Name _____

Address _____

City _____ State _____

Zip Code _____

REBATE

I should be receiving $ _____ for buying:

_____

I received my rebate on: _____

Phone # to call after _____ weeks: _____

Or online at: _____

MAIL ORDER

My mail order purchase was for:

_____

The cost was $ _____ and the order was

received on _____

Purchase Date: _____ Date Sent: _____

My Rebate/Mail Order was sent to:

Name _____

Address _____

City _____ State _____

Zip Code _____

REBATE

I should be receiving $_____ for buying:

_____

I received my rebate on: _____

Phone # to call after _____ weeks: _____

Or online at: _____

MAIL ORDER

My mail order purchase was for:

_____

The cost was $_____ and the order was

received on _____

▪▪▪▪▪▪▪▪▪▪▪▪▪▪▪▪▪▪▪▪▪▪▪▪▪▪▪▪▪▪▪▪▪▪▪▪▪

Purchase Date: _____ Date Sent _____

My Rebate/Mail Order was sent to:

Name _____

Address _____

City _____ State _____

Zip Code _____

REBATE

I should be receiving $_____ for buying:

_____

I received my rebate on: _____

Phone # to call after _____ weeks: _____

Or online at: _____

MAIL ORDER

My mail order purchase was for:

_____

The cost was $_____ and the order was

received on _____

Roger I. Goff

ABOUT THE AUTHOR

Roger Goff has been developing *The Original Rebate & Mail Order Tracker* for over 13 years. He found out a long time ago that Rebates and Mail orders, which you expect in the mail, don't always arrive. He started to keep records in a crude notebook and before long, he was pleased with his ability to check on overdue items. He started thinking that his crude notebook was harder to maintain then if he had a book to chart his information in. Today we can all benefit from the trial and errors of his 13-year adventure.

www.ingramcontent.com/pod-product-compliance
Lightning Source LLC
Chambersburg PA
CBHW052244290526
45785CB00016B/1278